MODERN
NOVEL WRITING

Engraved Portrait of William Beckford after Piat Joseph Sauvage (1744–1818)
From *The European Magazine and London Review*, 1797

MODERN NOVEL WRITING
OR THE ELEGANT ENTHUSIAST

WILLIAM BECKFORD

EDITED WITH AN INTRODUCTION AND NOTES BY
ROBERT J. GEMMETT

NONSUCH

For Hannah and Riley
'The world is all before them, where to choose'
Milton

This edition first published 2008

Nonsuch Publishing
Cirencester Road, Chalford, Stroud, Gloucestershire, GL6 8PE
www.nonsuch-publishing.com

Nonsuch Publishing is an imprint of NPI Media Group

British Library Cataloguing in Publication Data:
A catalogue record for this book is available from the British Library

ISBN 978 1 84588 608 0

Typesetting and origination by NPI Media Group
Printed in Great Britain

Contents

Foreword

William Beckford wrote *Modern Novel Writing* and *Azemia* against the background of the French Revolution and its traumatic aftermath, including the war between France and England that started in 1793. The revolutionary winds of change had a profound impact on British consciousness and produced inevitably both radical and reactionary responses to the shift towards more democratic paradigms. The response of the British government to the onset of new ideas and changes was to initiate a series of repressive measures clamping down on the freedoms of speech, writing and assembly, thereby preventing any form of dissent deemed dangerous to the welfare of the establishment and its ruling members. *Modern Novel Writing* begins by reacting against one of the literary trends of this period: the romantic sentimental novel, which flourished under these conditions by operating for the most part outside the discourse of political dissent. But, then, by the second volume of this novel, Beckford broadens his attack and utilizes the mask of anonymity to express himself more freely on some of the major social and political issues of the day. Despite the burlesque character of both novels, there is a serious level of discourse taking place, particularly evident in the attack he lodges against the Tory party, William Pitt and the dangerous insularity of the Prime Minister's political and social views. The seriousness of Beckford's satiric intent was reinforced, after the publication of *Modern Novel Writing*, by his own personal efforts to broker a peace single-handedly between France and England in 1797, operating completely outside normal channels of diplomacy. This bold effort may explain the stepped up attack in *Azemia* against the tyranny of the British government's autocratic policies and practices. Thus, while the dominant thrust of *Modern Novel Writing* consists of a strong attack against the shift of literary aesthetics towards the cultivation of sentimental excess over the dominance of reason, it gradually fuses the literary satire with concern about the climate of political intolerance and social injustice in England. This combination of elements is then carried forward and reinforced in *Azemia*. An astute observer of the shifting trends in Europe and England, Beckford perceived the rage for sentimental romances in his own country as absurdly escapist at a time when reason and common sense were called for to address the hard realities of war, poverty and political oppression that were traumatizing England in the 1790s. It is within the context of this intermingling of complex literary, social and political forces that Beckford's work can be best understood. The publication of modern editions of these two books, beginning with *Modern Novel Writing*, will hopefully demonstrate the breadth and multiple dimensions of Beckford's satire and promote a renewed critical assessment of these largely unknown works.

My decision to prepare critical editions of *Modern Novel Writing* and *Azemia* came about as result of research for my book, *Beckford's Fonthill: The Rise of a Romantic Icon*. It was during this period of study that I discovered unreported source material that provided additional confirmation of Beckford's authorship of these two satires. This led to an article published in the *Papers of the Bibliographical Society of America* (September 2004) and to my resurgence of interest in these works. With the passage of over 200 years since both books were published, I was struck by the fact that these two satiric novels have only been available in two facsimile reprint editions and neither one includes any textual notes or scholarly apparatus. George Robinson, the reputed 'king of the booksellers,' in partnership with his son George Jr and brother John, published the only English edition of *Modern Novel Writing* in 1796. A German translation was published two years later but very little is known about its existence or impact. Sampson Low of London published the first edition of *Azemia* in 1797, which enjoyed enough interest to come out in a second edition in 1798. A French edition by F. Soules appeared in 1808. These were the only original editions to have ever appeared. Deborah Griebel attempted to remedy the situation with her impressive doctoral dissertation, 'A Critical Edition of William Beckford's *Modern Novel Writing* and *Azemia*,' accepted for the degree by the University of Toronto in 1984, but it has never been published. Malcolm Jack edited an anthology of Beckford's prose in 1993, but included only limited excerpts of both satires. These new editions of *Modern Novel Writing* and *Azemia* will now join the corpus of scholarly editions of other literary works by this intriguing man of letters.

The completion of this book was facilitated by a number of individuals. First of all, I wish to express my indebtedness to Griebel's ground-breaking work on *Modern Novel Writing* and *Azemia*. Her dissertation is the most comprehensive critical and bibliographical study of both satires done so far. Her detective work in tracking down a number of literary sources Beckford used to satirize the rising tide of neo-Richardsonian sentimentalism in the eighteenth century was particularly helpful. Two other scholars who helped with the identification of source material were Frank Gees Black (*The Epistolary Novel in the Late Eighteenth Century*, 1940), who was the first person to identify Beckford's use of Samuel Richardson's well-known account of the attempted rape of Pamela, and Archibald Shepperson (*The Novel in Motley: A History of the Burlesque Novel in English*, 1936), the first individual to recognize the parody of Fielding's Man of the Hill story in *Tom Jones*.

Research on *Modern Novel Writing* and *Azemia* has been exceedingly limited. However, for this edition of *Modern Novel Writing*, I found André Parreaux's essay 'The Caliph and the Swinish Multitude' (1960) very useful as well as Boyd Alexander's chapter on 'France and Radicalism' in *England's Wealthiest Son* (1962), an important analysis of Beckford's social and political views.

A special thanks to my colleague Dr Austin Busch for his assistance with Beckford's Greek phrases and to Robert Gilliam for once again tracking down books and articles required to produce this edition.

Thanks also to Alan Sutton and Simon Hamlet of Nonsuch Publishing Ltd for supporting this project as a follow up to my revised edition of *Dreams, Waking Thoughts, and Incidents*, which they handsomely produced and published in 2006.

Finally, I wish to express my appreciation to the Beinecke Library, Yale University for providing me with a photocopy of Beckford's personal copy of *Modern Novel Writing*, which I used as a copy-text for this edition. For financial assistance in support of this project, I am once again grateful to the Scholarship Incentive Program sponsored by SUNY Brockport.

Introduction

In 1796 William Beckford published *Modern Novel Writing, or the Elegant Enthusiast; and Interesting Emotions of Arabella Bloomville. A Rhapsodical Romance; Interspersed with Poetry* under the pseudonym of Lady Harriet Marlow. This volume was followed almost immediately in 1797 by *Azemia: A Descriptive and Sentimental Novel. Interspersed with Pieces of Poetry* under the name of Jacquetta Agneta Mariana Jenks. Beckford linked the two volumes together as companion works by dedicating *Azemia* to 'The Right Honourable Lady Harriet Marlow.'

Curiously, very little information exists regarding the composition history of either book and no manuscripts have survived. There is a possible allusion to these satirical works in a letter Beckford wrote to his bookseller George Clarke in 1832, in which he asserted: 'If ever the world discovers the key of certain anonymous publications, it will find I have not been idle. All things considered, it had better not goad me to publish. Many would wince if I did."[1] Beckford also seems to be making a sly reference to his authorship of *Modern Novel Writing* in a hand-written note he left behind in his personal copy of this book now at the Bencicke Library at Yale, which has his initials 'W. B.' on a preliminary leaf followed by the words 'presentation copy from the divine authoress.'[2] Other evidence identifying Beckford as the author of these burlesques has rested on the testimony of the poets Thomas Moore and Samuel Rogers and that of Beckford's first biographer Cyrus Redding. After a three-day visit to Fonthill in 1817, Rogers recorded that Beckford read him two unpublished 'episodes to Vathek' and then noted that 'Beckford is the author of two burlesque novels, —*Azemia* and *The Elegant Enthusiast*, I have a copy of the former, which he

---

[1] *The Consummate Collector William Beckford's Letters to His Bookseller*, ed. R.J. Gemmett (Norwich: Michael Russell, 2000), 157.

[2] Howard Gotlieb, ed., *William Beckford of Fonthill Writer, Traveller, Collector, Caliph, 1760-1844* (New Haven: Yale University Library, 1960), 35.

presented to me.'³ Rogers was the source of Moore's own recorded statement in his personal journal indicating that he and Rogers 'talked of Beckford's two mock novels, Azemia & the Elegant Enthusiast.' Moore went on to describe a scene in *Modern Novel Writing* where 'the Heroine writes a Song, which she sings at a Masquerade, & which produces such an effect that my Lord Mahogany, in the character of a Mile-stone, bursts into tears.' He then adds: 'It is in *Azemia* that all the heroes & heroines are killed at the conclusion by a supper of stewed Lampreys.'⁴ While the former incident does occur in *Modern Novel Writing*, the catastrophe involving 'stewed Lampreys' is nowhere to be found in either novel. There is a similar incident that takes place in *Modern Novel Writing* involving the deaths of a number of people owing to a copper stew-pan in which some celery had been cooked. Moore's confusion here reveals that while he learned from Rogers of Beckford's authorship, he probably never read the books himself.

Cyrus Redding, who met Beckford during the period of time he was serving as editor of the *Bath Guardian* (1834–5) and then later became his biographer, was, as in the case of Rogers, another important source of attribution. Redding noted that Beckford's taste for the burlesque manifested itself at an early age when he wrote and published *Biographical Memoirs of Extraordinary Painters* (1780). 'In the present instance, at a more advanced age,' Redding explained, 'seeing the absurdity and bombast that passed current for fine writing, and remarkably sarcastic as he was, he published in 1796 and 1797, two works, each in two small volumes.' He then identified *Modern Novel Writing* and *Azemia* as the titles and proceeded to reproduce a significant amount of the first novel with some notes and occasional commentary as illustrative of Beckford's satiric style.⁵

While evidence for the attribution of authorship for these two novels has rested on Rogers, Moore, and Redding and Beckford's own tantalizing allusions to it, there exists some additional support from contemporary writers that has recently been reported.⁶ The first is an article in *The Ladies' Monthly Museum* in 1824. This magazine was running a biographical series devoted to 'eccentric characters' and included Beckford as one of them in their February issue of that

---

³ *Recollections of the Table-Talk of Samuel Rogers* (New York: Appleton, 1856), 215. Rogers's copy of *Azemia* showed up in the Christie and Manson sale of his books in 1856 as lot 1737. It is now located in the rare book library of UCLA, bearing the inscription 'S. Rogers, Esqr.' in the first volume.

⁴ *The Journal of Thomas Moore*, ed. Wilfred Dowden (Newark: University of Delaware Press, 1983), I: 70.

⁵ Cyrus Redding, *Memoirs of William Beckford of Fonthill* (London: Charles Skeet, 1859), II: 162-3.

⁶ See R. J. Gemmett, 'William Beckford's Authorship of *Modern Novel Writing* and *Azemia*,' *The Papers of the Bibliographical Society of America*, 98 (September, 2004): 313-25. I have incorporated a good portion of this article in this introduction.

year. Beckford was enjoying a great deal of attention in the press during this time largely because of Fonthill Abbey and the two major 'public views' which took place there in 1822 and 1823. The anonymous writer of this biography explains that while the creation of Beckford's Fonthill and his subsequent 'Saxon tower' at Lansdown, Bath were the primary reasons for his inclusion in the gallery of eccentrics, he had also distinguished himself in the field of literature with the publication of *Vathek*. The writer then went on to note that there were other publications attributed to his authorship that 'though less known, are hardly less distinguished, for the traits of talent which they display, and the peculiar satirical turn of mind which uniformly seems to actuate the author.' The article mentions *Biographical Memoirs of Extraordinary Painters* and then *Modern Novel Writing* and *Azemia*. 'Both these latter publications,' the author wrote, 'were intended as satires on the sentimental style of novel writing; a species of composition once very popular, but now deservedly fallen into contempt.'[7]

Another source for identifying Beckford as the author of these two novels is John Mitford, editor of the *Gentleman's Magazine*, 1834-50, and of the works of Thomas Gray, John Milton and other poets. Mitford had a high regard for Beckford as a writer and publicly praised his literary talents in major reviews of *Italy, with Sketches of Spain and Portugal* and *Recollections of an Excursion to the Monasteries of Alcobaça and Batalha* in the *Gentleman's Magazine*.[8] In Mitford's unpublished recollections written in 1844, consisting of anecdotes on leading figures of his time, he reveals having seen a 'Novel written by "Beckford," called Azemia,' and that he once owned *Modern Novel Writing*, which he describes as 'a Novel of Beckford's, in which the Party take Salts at Night, & write Sonnets in the Morning. Ld Mahogany sheds tears & is turnd into a Milestone, and the whole die of a dish of Lampreys stewed in a Copper Sauce Pan.'[9] Mitford comes up with the true copper pot in his account, but the inclusion of the fanciful Lamphrey stew indicates that his source of information was Moore since he repeats the poet's flawed description.

One of the most reliable sources for establishing Beckford as the author of these two burlesques, however, is John Britton, a leading publicist of the Gothic revival movement in England and author of one of the descriptive

---

[7] 'Biography of Eccentric Characters. William Beckford,' *The Ladies' Monthly Museum*, 19 (February 1824): 71. How this writer obtained this information is not possible to determine since the identity of the author is not known and even the name of the editor of the journal for this year remains a mystery.

[8] *Gentleman's Magazine*, 2 (August, September 1834): 115-21, 234-41.

[9] John Hodgkin's transcription of Mitford's notes on Beckford from British Museum Add. MSS. 32.567. For Hodgkin's notes, see MS. Eng. Misc., Bodleian Library, e. 198, fol. 36.

accounts of Fonthill Abbey. Britton was impressed to the point of intimidation with Beckford's intellectual capabilities and range of knowledge about a variety of subjects. He told Beckford in 1835 that when he first met him in 1799, he was 'astonished and terrified' by his 'splendours & powers.'[10] Britton often made it a point to discover the names of the authors of anonymous books and articles that appeared in the press. In the unpublished correspondence between Beckford and Britton at the Bodleian Library, Britton makes some significant remarks about *Azemia* wherein he appears to be attempting to confirm Beckford's authorship. Near the end of a letter to Beckford in November 1823, Britton writes that he was impressed with the book: 'We have lately caught the fair "Azemia" and have derived much risibility over some of its burlesques. It contains some truly original & *striking* pages. Its author seems to have read every thing & knows every thing. I hope *she* has produced other works for the benefit of readers.' Beckford's response exists in draft form, but he plays along with Britton's coyness: 'Upon the subject of the fair Author of Azemia ... I am as ignorant as yourself whether she has produced or is likely to produce any other works for inst[ruction] or amuse[ment].'[11] Finally, in Britton's letter to Beckford of 27 November 1823, he adds a postscript in which he says that Sampson Low, the publisher of *Azemia*, told him that Charlotte Smith was the author, to which Britton responds: 'I will not believe it, tho' the Compositor & even the Devil himself swore to it.'[12] It is clear that Britton ultimately believed that Beckford was the author because in the sale of his books at Southgate's in June 1832, he listed his personal copy of *Azemia* as Beckford's work.[13]

Both books are now very rare with only a limited number of copies known to exist.[14] The rarity of *Modern Novel Writing*, moreover, is compounded by the existence of variant copies of the first edition and of two copies that bear

---

[10] ALS, 13 July 1835, MS. Beckford, Bodleian Library, c. 27, fols. 32-3.

[11] MS. Beckford, Bodleian Library, c. 27, fols. 18-20.

[12] *Ibid.*, fols. 22-3. Guy Chapman cites this passage but omits mention of Britton's earlier statements about *Azemia*. See *A Bibliography of William Beckford of Fonthill*, ed. Guy Chapman and John Hodgkin (London: Constable, 1930), 47.

[13] Lot 376 of the sale: 'Jenks' (J.A.M.) *Azemia, a Novel*, by W. Beckford, 2 vol. 1798.' [second edition].

[14] Twelve copies have been located so far: 4 copies at the Beinecke Library, Yale University, 1 at the Bodleian Library, Oxford University, 2 at the British Library, 1 at Princeton University, 1 at Harvard University, 1 at UCLA, 1 copy listed in Bernard Quaritch (catalogue 1132, October 1990), and 1 included in the sale of H. Bradley Martin's library in New York on 30 April 1990. To provide some idea of the rarity of these two books: the hammer price for Martin's copy of *Modern Novel Writing* was $8,000 while *Azemia* sold for $8,500. The catalogue price for the Quaritch copy was $20,000. See also section on 'Textual Notes' for additional details.

dedication pages with a date earlier than 1796, the year normally ascribed to its publication. In their bibliography of Beckford's works, Guy Chapman and John Hodgkin provide a description of one of the rare oddities using Hodgkin's personal copy, which is now part of the Bodleian Library collection. The title page for each volume bears the date 'MDCCXCVI' in accord with the dedication page in the first volume that concludes with the date 'March 31st, 1796.' At variance with this date, however, is the dedication bound into volume II which contains the date 'Sept. 21st, 1795,' raising the possibility of the existence of an earlier issue of the first edition.[15] But, since all other existing copies of the book contained the 1796 date, it has been assumed that this variant dedication was a cancelled pre-publication state that had somehow survived and was bound into Hodgkin's copy as a curiosity that would be of interest to a collector.

The publication history of *Modern Novel Writing* suddenly became more complicated when a new copy surfaced in a Bernard Quaritch catalogue issued in 1990.[16] This specimen in two volumes, 12mo, bound in contemporary sheep with dark green morocco labels and gilt bands and numerals on the spines, was described as the 'unique, hitherto unrecorded, first issue of the first edition' published in 1795. The catalogue description went on to point out that all of the other copies in existence were, in fact, 'examples of a secondary issue, with re-set title and dedication pages dated 1796.' This copy bore in earlier settings an undated title page and a dedication page in the preliminaries of the first volume with the date 'Sept. 21st, 1795,' which led them to conclude that it is 'probable that the book was originally issued late in 1795 (our copy) and reissued in April 1796 (all others).' This example, they believed, helps to explain how the Hodgkin copy at the Bodleian—'clearly an unintended freak'—came into existence. A journal article followed thereafter that provided additional information: 'The titles of each volume are in a different, almost certainly earlier setting from those in all other known copies: there is no date, and the epigraph from Pope just above the imprint is in a slightly larger type than that employed for the 1796 dated issue, and not quite so well centred—the text extending slightly to the left of the "L" in "Lady Harriet." The eighth line in the dated issue ends "Romance;", and in this undated issue ends "Romance." in volume I, and "Romance," in volume II—although perhaps the apparent full stop in volume I is in fact a comma, badly printed.'[17]

---

[15] Chapman and Hodgkin, 46.

[16] Bernard Quaritch catalogue 1132, 'English Books & Manuscripts,' item 7, pp. 5-7, issued in October 1990.

[17] Arthur Freeman, 'William Beckford's *Modern Novel Writing*, 1795-6: Two Issues, "Three States,"' *Book Collector*, 41 (Spring 1992): 69-71.

Unfortunately, there are problems with both reports in their attempt to promote the existence of a first issue published prior to 1796 in that neither one addresses complications posed by internal and external evidence that preclude the possibility of an earlier appearance of the novel. For example, there are a number of references in the second volume of *Modern Novel Writing* to the Treasonable and Seditious Practices and Seditious Meetings Acts, which were not passed until 18 December 1795. In at least three of these references, Beckford addresses these repressive measures in the past tense, that is, as having already been enacted (pp. 144, 150, 183). As in the case of the 'Humble Address to the Doers of that Excellent and Impartial Review, called *The British Critic*,' which appears at the end of the novel, Beckford writes ironically: 'I perfectly approve of the two restraining bills which have lately passed into laws.' It is also worth noting that all of the recorded initial reviews of *Modern Novel Writing* identify 1796 as the publishing date with the earliest review identified so far appearing in August of that year. The most significant piece of evidence, however, is the publisher's announcement of the book's publication in the *The Times*, which establishes the publication date as 14 June 1796. The advertisement read:

> This day is published, in 2 Vols. price 7s. boards,
>   Modern Novel Writing; or, The elegant Enthusiast,
> and interesting Emotions of Arabella Bloomville; a
> Rhapsodical Romance, interspersed with Poetry.
>   By the Right Hon. Lady HARRIET MARLOW.
> Printed for G. G. and J. Robinson, Paternoster-row.[18]

In view of this evidence, Cyrus Redding's statement that both 'burlesque novels were written at Fonthill before the decease of his mother in 1798,' has to be considered inaccurate.[19] It is known that Beckford had not been in residence at Fonthill since November 1793, when he left for an extended stay in Portugal. He did not return to England until 20 June 1796.[20] It would have to be the case then that only *Azemia* could have been written at Fonthill and that *Modern Novel Writing* had to have been completed in Portugal. These particulars, therefore, suggest another explanation for the existence of the

---

[18] *The Times*, 14 June 1796, p. 2b. I have also not found a publisher's announcement for *Modern Novel Writing* during the period running from 21 September to 31 December 1795, as one would expect if the book were published then.

[19] Redding, II: 223.

[20] See the notice about Beckford's arrival in *The Times*, 30 June 1796, p. 3.

1795 dedication page. It is conceivable that the publisher, Robinson, had the first volume in hand by late 1795, prepared the title and dedication pages, but because of a delay in receiving the second volume in a final form authorized by Beckford, he then cancelled these pages and re-set new title and dedication pages after volume two was received sometime after 18 December 1795 and before 14 June 1796. To try to make a case for the receipt and publication of the two volumes as we know the book today within a time frame of 13 days in December would be unrealistic if not impossible. This would also help to explain why the Quaritch copy has no date on the title pages. In this sequence of events, the copy in the Bodleian Library, as described by Chapman, would not change its status as a first issue variant copy. It should be pointed out, however, that the Bodleian copy is not a variant simply on the basis of the 'freak' dedication page bound in volume two, as Chapman and Hodgkin described it. It does contain substantive internal changes when compared to other extant copies placing it in a category of a corrected copy.[21] Until it is possible to examine the text of the Quaritch copy, one would have to conclude that it is either a chrysalis or pre-publication copy or another anomaly like the Hodgkin specimen, with the undated title pages and 1795 dedication page bound in with a published copy of 1796.[22]

II

Reminiscent of the satiric style of his first published book, *Biographical Memoirs of Extraordinary Painters*, both *Modern Novel Writing* and *Azemia* were designed in part to ridicule the sentimental and sensational novels of the day, particularly the productions of William Lane's Minerva Press. Elizabeth Hervey, Beckford's half-sister, is usually identified as the principal object of attack for her works in the sentimental vein, particularly *Melissa and Marcia* (1788) and *Louisa* (1790). It is clear that Beckford was also thinking of the

---

[21] The most comprehensive bibliographical discussion of these two novels to date is Deborah Griebel's doctoral dissertation, 'A Critical Edition of William Beckford's *Modern Novel Writing* and *Azemia*,' University of Toronto, 1984. As part of her invaluable research, she collated nine copies of the English edition of *Modern Novel Writing* and found textual variants in four 'corrected' copies (Rogers's copy at UCLA, PR 4091.m72, the British library copy, 12614.bb 15, the Hodgkin copy at Oxford, 12 Θ 1164-1165, and the Yale copy, B388/796/copy 3). She used the Hodgkin copy at Oxford for her edition as a 'fully corrected text.' I have used Beckford's personal copy of *Modern Novel Writing* (Yale, copy 3) for this edition and provide a list of his changes in the section on 'Textual Notes' at the end of this volume.

[22] Unfortunately, I have not been able to identify the current owner or location of the Quaritch copy to be able to conduct a comparison.

more general proliferation of sentimental and Gothic novels in the 1780s and 1790s, particularly if they were authored by women. Towards the end of *Azemia*, he mentions the authors parodied, starting with three males, Samuel Richardson, Henry Fielding, and Richard Cumberland and then identifying a number of female authors, including Francis Burney, Ann Radcliffe, Sophia Lee, Charlotte Smith, Helen Maria Williams, Elizabeth Inchbald, Elizabeth Gunning, Susanna Gunning, Hester Piozzi and Mary Robinson. The specific works he used as sources for *Modern Novel Writing* included Richardson's *Pamela* (1740) and Fielding's *Tom Jones* (1749). Other sources he relied upon were the following works by women: Lady Cassandra Hawke's *Julia de Gramont* (1788), Elizabeth Hervey's *Melissa and Marcia* (1788), Ann Radcliffe's *The Castles of Athlin and Dunbayne* (1789), Charlotte Smith's *Celestina* (1791), and Mary Robinson's *Vancenza; or, The Dangers of Credulity* (1792). Female authors were prominent as sources in *Modern Novel Writing* because they were the ones who carried the torch of Richardsonian sentimentalism at this time, and well-known as the 'scribblomaniacs' of the new gospel of feeling. In 1821 Beckford revealed how he felt about their works. 'It might be as well,' he wrote, 'if instead of weaving historical romances the super-literary ladies of the present period would pass a little more of their time at cross stitch and yabble stitch. We should gain some pretty chair and screen covers and lose little by not being tempted to pore over the mazes of their interminable scribbleations.'[23]

In *Modern Novel Writing* Beckford manages to highlight almost all of the flagrant excesses of the neo-Richardsonians of the day. Instead of a carefully articulated plot, for example, he presents the reader with a patchwork of incidents—poorly constructed, crowded with irrelevant detail and absent of any unity. As in the novels he parodies, the characters tend to appear and disappear without purpose or meaning. Bombast replaces natural speech for the purpose of giving expression to the false sentiment and overstrained emotions that pervade the book. There is a painfully familiar heroine, Arabella Bloomville, who can swoon in the face of indecency. Lord Mahogany, the pursuing villain, is a comic version of Samuel Richardson's Lovelace who ultimately expires while giving a speech. The hero, Henry Lambert, with his bright hazel eyes, a nose 'inclined to the Grecian' and a complexion 'fair as alabaster,' is the stylized Man of Feeling. Henry's problem is also not without precedent: he experiences periods of separation from his object of love and then total paralysis when he sees her. Complications arise when Arabella finds out that she is the daughter of a Countess, but as luck would have it, Henry is likely to receive a title himself

---

[23] Gotlieb, 64.

and hence is emboldened to ask for her hand in marriage, which provides the occasion for one of the most rhapsodic speeches in the novel:

O matchless effervescence of human happiness, divine empress of my soul, I have languished for ages to behold thee, I have been burnt up and consumed by the unquenchable fire of exhaustless passion. Every moment that passed, seemed to me to have the duration of a century. The sports of the field were vain in thy absence. I seemed like a forsaken doe on the banks of the Tigris. The golden glory of the sun when darting his meridian splendor on the sycamore shade, had no solace for my distracted heart. In sleep, the dainty visions of thy loveliness, played on my secluded senses, and irritated my hopes to the madness of despair. There was no music in the murmuring of the silver rivulet that babbled through the flowery brake; the pale moon glared on me with the dimness of death. O Queen of all my wishes, O incomparable Arabella, O thou most beautiful of the human race, what will become of me, if your frowns should fall upon me! one kiss from thy sweet lips would raise me to a height of joy, that the proudest earthly potentate never yet experienced in his gilded palace, or his outrageous ministers in the wide plunderings of official power. Wilt thou be mine, wilt thou bless thy Henry by accepting his proffered hand? Wilt thou become myself, the chief portion of my being, the light of my eyes, the rapture of my soul?

The two lovers do unite in marriage and, as the title for Henry does materialize, they live happily ever after as 'Lord and Lady Laughable.' In this manner, through the consistent employment of these stock characteristics, Beckford demonstrates the flaws of sentimental fiction that had become so formulaic during the 1780s and 1790s.

Beckford also employs parody throughout to achieve his satiric goals. Sometimes, he draws upon specific scenes that would be well known to the reading public, such as the famous attempted rape scene in Richardson's *Pamela* and 'The Man of the Hill' episode in Fielding's *Tom Jones*. In the chapter entitled 'The Struggles of Virtue Prevail,' Beckford's recreates in close detail the attempted rape of Pamela but substitutes a wicked Marchioness for Mrs. Jewkes and Lord Mahogany for Mr B. The victim of the scheme is Arabella's friend, 'the valuable suffering Amelia.' In a recent study of *Pamela*, two Richardsonian scholars consider Beckford's adaptation to be highly effective: 'Beckford deftly perverts the already fervid eroticism of Richardson's notorious scene by making the marchioness an enthusiastic collaborator in the would-be rape, rather than the servant in her master's pay. Beckford also heightens the disparity in rank between Pamela and Mr B. by giving titles to both of Amelia's persecutors.' [24] To achieve the comic effect here, Beckford counts on the public's familiarity with this scene, knowing that Richardson's book continued to be widely read in the 1790s. Beckford's parody of Fielding's Man of the Hill is not as detailed but is equally effective. Fielding had his famous misanthropic recluse resign from society in order to contemplate the divine character of the universe and ponder the ultimate question as to why a benevolent God would create such a vile creature as man; Beckford deflates Fielding's account by having his recluse abandon human society for the purpose of engaging in such 'deep researches' as the calculation of the 'succession of seconds passed since the creation of the world,' the 'average number of hairs that grow upon the heads of all mankind' and of 'how many millions of words womankind utter every twenty-four hours throughout all the world.' Part of the humour of this conversion derives from the way Beckford turns one of Fielding's own comic techniques against him and undercuts the serious role the interpolated story is supposed to play in developing the theme of natural benevolence in *Tom Jones*.

At other times, Beckford actually borrows passages and sometimes entire chapters from existing novels as if he were providing the reader with the original text to illustrate a point in the manner of a contemporary review. What is unusual about this method is that he holds up a mirror to a generic literary landscape and does not identify the specific source he uses. He relies, instead, on the reader to recognize the passage, as in the case of Elizabeth Hervey, who upon reading the description of Lord Mahogany's estate in the chapter on 'Captivating Scenery' in *Modern Novel Writing* recognized immediately that it came from her own book, *Melissa and Marcia or the Two Sisters* (1788). As the poet Thomas Moore explained, reporting a conversation with Samuel Rogers, Hervey was quite aware of the borrowing: 'Why, I vow and protest, here is my grotto.' [25] In his address to the reviewers of *The British Critic* at the end of *Modern Novel Writing*, Beckford admits to these borrowings from 'our most modern writers' and asks for forgiveness for so 'venial an offence,' noting that the passages transplanted, 'which shew to disadvantage in their new situations, were not inserted with a design of depreciating their excellence, but merely to display that happy intricacy of style and sentiment, without which no novel can have a just claim', to the notice and approbation of the worthy 'doers' of *The British Critic*. 'With all humility,' he adds, 'I am free to

---

[24] Thomas Keymer and Peter Sabor, *Pamela in the Marketplace Literary Controversy and Print Culture in Eighteenth-Century Britain and Ireland* (Cambridge: Cambridge University Press, 2005), 210.

[25] Dowden, I: 70.

assert, that some of those extracts which unfortunately in my little work may seem ludicrous and absurd, possess great beauty and propriety as connected with their original combinations.'

In his biography, Redding provided information about Beckford's intent in writing these novels. He explained that though Beckford praised Hervey's novels, particularly *Louisa* (1790), he found them to be reflective of the bad taste of the times and written in the vein of those works being promoted by the leader of this literary rage, the 'Minerva press in Leadenhall Street.' 'It is no doubt a singular and degrading thing in literature,' he wrote, 'that it should have become, in the department of novel writing, and continue to be, as changeable in its fashion as the cut of the ladies' dresses, or the fashionable music. In the period of the Leadenhall Street reign, of which the present generation [in 1859] can know little, just as in those days which succeeded it down to this hour, the style, mode of thinking, and sentimentality in novels, underwent continual mutations. A comparison of the novels of Mary Robinson, or Charlotte Smith, Ann Radcliff, and Monk Lewis, with those which succeeded by Scott, would explain the differences, and still more those of the present hour, set in comparison with them.' [26] According to Redding, it was Beckford's sense that the growing taste for this undisciplined and extravagant style of writing was corrupting the standards of good literature.

Beckford did not limit examples of sentimental extravagance to the genre of prose. The excess of sentimentality in prose was equally matched in the 1780s and 90s by enthusiasts in verse. An exquisite type of poetry, which is scattered throughout the *Modern Novel Writing*, is representative of the conventions of the sentimental school:

> Love is a soft, involuntary flame,
>   Beyond the pow'r of language to express;
> That throws resistless magic o'er the frame,
>   And leads to boundless pleasure or distress.

Among the leaders of this new vogue of sensibility were Charlotte Smith, Mary Robinson, and Anna Seward. All three writers had a considerable impact on the evolving aesthetics of Romanticism. Robinson, who was already a celebrity because of her affair with the Prince of Wales, published her first collection of poems in 1791 with the impressive support of almost 600 subscribers. She then followed this collection with her 'legitimate' (after Petrarch) sonnet sequence *Sappho and Phaon* in 1796, which reinforced her reputation as 'the English Sappho.' [27] Anna Seward,

---

[26] Redding, II: 161-2.

a prolific writer of sonnets, published *Louisa* in 1784, an entire sentimental novel published in verse that was sufficiently successful to reach five editions by 1792. The popularity of Smith's *Elegiac Sonnets* (1784), moreover, was an additional testimony to the intense interest in emotional verse at the time. Credited with the revival of the moribund sonnet tradition in the eighteenth century, the technicalities of the Shakespearian or 'illegitimate' form she employed may have been of less interest to the reading public than the dominance of the elegiac mood that permeated her works. Despite Seward's criticism that they were 'ever-lasting lamentables' and 'hackneyed scraps of dismality,' Smith's sonnet collection ran through eleven English editions, enjoyed an American readership, and received accolades from such luminaries as Wordsworth, Coleridge and Sir Walter Scott.[28] Beckford draws attention to Smith's poetry of anguished grief when in the novel the heroine Arabella calls upon the aid of the 'tender muse' to find relief from her melancholia in the following example of 'her exquisite poetical powers:'

Sonnet.

When sorrow's humblest haunts reflect the beam
    That patient virtue scatters o'er the plain,
No wanton zephyr curls the languid stream,
    No melting woodlark wakes the warbled strain.

For me, alas! beset with storms of woe,
    Where plaintive ecchoes die upon the gale,
May the still voice of agony bestow,
    The softest requiem to the rustic vale.

O! my lov'd Henry! shouldst thou ever hear
    How feebly flows the meditated lay,
While the pale moonshine gilds the checquer'd sphere;
    Thou might'st again the distant theme display,

Might'st drop th' appropriate plaudit of a tear,
    And whisper sweetness to the charms of May.

---

[27] Paula Byrne, *Perdita The Literary, Theatrical, Scandalous Life of Mary Robinson* (New York: Random House), 258.

[28] *The Letters of Anna Seward Written between the Years 1784 and 1807* (Edinburgh, 1811), II: 287. See also Raymond D. Havens, *The Influence of Milton on English Poetry* (New York: Russell & Russell, 1961), 503.

Other leaders of this literary fad included a coterie of poets called the Della Cruscans whose primary contributors were Robert Merry, Bertie Greatheed, William Parsons, and Hester Lynch Piozzi. Influenced by the emerging cult of feeling in Europe and by a desire for free poetical expression, they began their collaboration with the publication of the *Florence Miscellany* in 1785, when they were English residents in Italy and Merry was a member of the Academia della Crusca in Florence, which gave the group its name.[29] Their poems became known for their superficial display of emotion and gained in popularity when they found outlets in England in Edward Topham's *The World* and the *European Magazine*. The rage reached its height when Merry, using the pen name Della Crusca, and Mrs Cowley, writing under the name Aunt Matilda, began an idealized 'romantic' correspondence in Topham's newspaper that continued for two years and caused a host of followers and sometimes oppressive imitations.

The Della Cruscan's arch enemy was William Gifford, a vitriolic critic who receives considerable attention in *Modern Novel Writing*. Gifford, the Tory satirist and future editor of the *Anti-Jacobin Weekly*, described the Della Cruscan school of poetry in the *Baviad* (1791) as 'the ropy drivel of rheumatic brains.'[30]. He returned to the subject in the *Mæviad* (1795) where he expanded his criticism to include contemporary dramatists. The works of the Della Cruscans, he believed, were orgies of sentiment, filled with 'noise,' 'nonsense,' 'false glare,' and 'incongruous images.' What was striking about Gifford's attack was his passion for vindictiveness and his strong *ad hominem* assaults. It is Gifford's bitterness that Beckford emphasizes when introducing him as 'a little sour looking fellow, but prodigiously powerful with his pen, for he is desperately severe.' Elsewhere, Beckford refers to a performance by Gifford entitled 'Upon the pleasures of malignity.' While he shared Gifford's dislike for the overblown emotions of the Della Cruscans and even targeted them himself for derision in *Azemia*, he felt that Gifford was a talentless writer who could not write a genuine line of poetry himself. He portrays him as an insufferable pedant whose literary achievements were mired in mediocrity.

Beckford's strength as a satirist is no more apparent than in his treatment of Gifford's 'Ode to the Rev. John Ireland,' which appeared as a footnote to the *Mæviad*. Beckford's transcribes extracts from the poem almost word for word, but then creates an extensive set of footnotes for them to mock—in a very effective parody—Gifford's habit of adding elaborate notes to his own texts that were

---

[29] For useful information about the rise and decline of the Della Cruscans, see W. N. Hargreaves-Mawdsley, *The English Della Cruscans and their Time, 1783-1828* (The Hague: Martinus Nijhoff, 1967).

[30] *The Baviad and Mæviad* (London, 1798), 46.

entirely self serving and that were intended to impress the reader with a show of learning. In addition, Beckford may have spied the same vein of sentimentality that Gifford ridicules in the writings of others in the critic's own Ode. Writing about his friendship with John Ireland, Gifford explained: 'I only seek, in language void of art,/ To ope my breast, and pour out all my heart;/ And boastful of thy various worth , to tell,/ How long we lov'd, and thou canst add, HOW WELL!' [31] The sentimental strain is also apparent in Gifford's relationship with the painter John Hoppner, called Sam Slybore in the text. In the uncorrected versions of *Modern Novel Writing*, Beckford has Gifford refer to the portrait painter as '*my* Hopner,' [32] a direct allusion to the lines from the Ireland ode that Gifford wrote in celebration of their friendship: 'Thou too, MY HOPPNER! ... Who long have seen thy merits, long have loved,/ Yet loved in silence, lest the rout should say/ Too partial friendship tuned th' applausive lay.' [33] Redding may have echoed Beckford's own sentiments when he described Gifford 'as a man raised from obscurity by individual kindness, and then, as narrow minds always incline, directed to exalt his own importance at the cost of minds far higher than his own genius, and less, infinitely less, tortuous in conduct.' [34]

Modern Novel Writing has other targets in view besides sentimental fiction and verse. London's fashionable society also comes under attack. Part of the explanation for this assault stems from Beckford's involvement in a public scandal in 1784 in which he was accused of having a sexual liaison with the young heir of Powderham Castle, William Courtenay. While the charges in the news-sheets were never substantiated, he became a marked figure in British society. The situation was complicated by the fact that he was also seeking a English peerage at the same time through Lord Chancellor Thurlow, which might have been successful had it not been for the public accusation, considered a capital offence at this time. The significant player behind the scene was Lord Loughborough, husband of Courtenay's sister, Charlotte, and a man who already harboured a personal dislike for Beckford. Loughborough considered Thurlow his major political rival and was jealous of Beckford's potential for a peerage with the Lord Chancellor's support. Destroying Beckford would be a way of undermining his political enemy as well.

---

[31] *Ibid.*, 140.

[32] From the uncorrected copies of *Modern Novel Writing* at the Beinecke Library, Yale University, (B88, Duke of Bedford's copy, and B388.79 copies 1 and 2).

[33] *The Mæviad*, 140; 142.

[34] Redding, II: 199-200.

The aftermath of social isolation naturally resulted in feelings of resentment against the group of people who once sought his company and ultimately against the political establishment which distanced themselves from him. Where he had been lionized as a brilliant figure in the houses of Ladies Lucan, Home, Clarges, Archer, Mary Duncan and Mrs Montague, he was not now allowed to cross their thresholds. To complicate matters, the shadow of suspicion persisted in the mind of the public and dogged him for the rest of his life. It began the process of marginalization that prevented him from being taken seriously even to the present day. It also led to his own solipsistic withdrawal into a reclusive life at his Fonthill estate in Wiltshire and later in Lansdown Crescent, Bath.

Consequently, *Modern Novel Writing* provided Beckford with a catharsis for some of the malaise he experienced over his treatment as a pariah and an opportunity to strike back in a public forum. He began by targeting two of the most prominent hostesses in the London social scene, Elizabeth Montagu and Hester Thrale Piozzi. Montagu, the Queen of the Bluestocking set, appears as Mrs Maltrever. Montagu, who was Beckford's neighbour in Portman Square, had distinguished herself as the leader of the intellectual salon culture of women in London. She had dedicated herself to the support of female education and the encouragement of women writers. Through the vehicle of Maltrever, Beckford alters her role by providing the opposite advice to a young woman in the story, telling her to avoid 'that sort of petulance and incongruity, which is but too often the result of ill-placed ambition, and a desire to distinguish herself in literary composition.' Beckford then mocks Piozzi under the name Mrs De Malthe, a veiled reference to her first husband's 'malt' factory or brewery in Southwark.[35] Following the Powderham scandal, Piozzi dubbed Beckford the 'Professor of Pæderasty' and called *Vathek* a 'mad Book' by a 'mad Author,' noting that his *'favourite Propensity'* was visible throughout particularly in the 'luscious Descriptions given to Gulchenrouz.' [36] Beckford attacks her for her shallow social obsessions and as a self righteous religious and political conservative, who was 'fully and properly persuaded that kings can do no wrong, and that they were authorized by heaven to massacre and plunder their own subjects, and to desolate the world at their pleasure.' He also highlights her habit of pretentiously displaying her erudition in public and in her written works, which she would often laid with 'scraps' of Latin and Greek. At one point, he has De Malthe give a speech that

---

[35] Mary Hyde, *The Thrales of Streatham Park* (Cambridge: Harvard University Press, 1977), 1.

[36] *Thraliana The Diary of Mrs. Hester Lynch Thrale 1776-1809*, ed. Katharine C. Balderston (Oxford: Clarendon Press, 1951), II: 799; 969.

illustrates this tediously pedantic and convoluted style, which, in effect, is a clever parody of Piozzi's *British Synonymy*, a book she published in 1794.

Beckford also devotes considerable space to political satire directed against the Tory party, William Pitt and the members of his administration. Interspersed among the nonsense in *Modern Novel Writing* are attacks on the British government's policy of war against France that had been raging since 1793. Beckford singles out by name such political cronies of Pitt as the President of the Council, Lord Mansfield, the Secretary of State for War, Henry Dundas, the 'humane' William Windham, who was known for his strong resistance to any peace negotiations with France, and the Foreign Secretary, Lord Grenville, a leading supporter of repressive domestic legislation to maintain order in Britain. The 'great' George Rose, Secretary Treasury, is also featured who, with Grenville, Mansfield, and Windham, stood aloof from the consequences of the agricultural decline and the widespread domestic distress. These 'sublime personages' seemed to be 'the happiest of men, in spite of the high price of bread, and the encreasing weight of taxes,' since they had, as Beckford observes, no effect on them.

Beckford's strongest attack against the war is embedded in a speech given by Lord Mahogany in the throes of his final illness. Amidst his incoherent ravings, reminiscent of George III's intervals of madness, he reveals his deep guilt for supporting the war in the House of Lords: 'I might have given my vote for peace! but O! 'twas war, war, war! how they bleed! thousands, ten thousands dead! such a waste of murder! … O! this cursed war—I voted for it—how it burns my brain … O! conscience, conscience! … alas! the war is mine … Bottle up the war in a corn-field, and put my vote in hell.' In another section, Beckford satirises Pitt's government for such repressive measures as the Treasonable and Seditious Practices Act and Seditious Meetings Act of 1795, which aimed at frustrating the legitimate complaints of the people:

> Then the people assembled in great multitudes to complain, and petitioned their oppressors to grant them some relief, but they found none, their just remonstrances were deemed seditious and treasonable, and the men who had thus seized the reigns of authority, published an order forbidding all persons to assemble, or even to murmur …

These acts, when carried into execution, ensured a 'dead silence throughout the nation.' Order and tranquillity were restored, but England had now become, as Beckford characterizes it, 'THE ISLAND OF MUM.'

Beckford sets up for specific disdain prominent individuals who are public supporters of Pitt and the official party line. One of these individuals was John

Reeves, a well-known government propagandist and informer. Reeves founded the Society for Preserving Liberty and Property against Republicans and Levellers in 1792. It was their goal to suppress seditious publications and to silence anti-establishment sentiments. Redding once described Reeves as 'the over-officious tool of the court,' who believed that if parliaments were destroyed, the king would remain as an all-sufficient authority.[37] Beckford links the 'immaculate Mr. Reeves' as a sympathizer with the views of Revd Robert Nares ('so renowned ... for his love of royalty, and detestation of liberty') and Revd William Beloe, who appear under the names Squares and Bilbo in the book. They were founding editors of the conservative monthly, *The British Critic,* which began publication in 1793 as a voice against revolutionary views and liberal discourse. It was believed that this journal was able to be launched initially because of backing from Pitt's secret service money and Tory churchmen subscriptions.[38]

At the end of *Modern Novel Writing*, Beckford includes 'An Humble Address to the Doers of that Excellent and Impartial Review Called The British Critic' in which he provides a sustained piece of irony mocking support of their establishment ideology in a text that alludes to the opposing philosophies of Edmund Burke and Thomas Paine:

> To your virtues, liberality, and candour, the whole nation can bear testimony, for I defy the most impudent of your detractors to shew a single instance amongst all your writings, where you have spoken favorably of any work that was base enough to vindicate the hoggish herd of the people, that was mean enough to object to any measures of the present wise and incorruptible administration, or that was cowardly enough to censure the just and necessary war in which the nation is now so fortunately engaged. No, ye worthy magistrates of the mind! you have exerted your civil jurisdiction with meritorious perseverance ...
>
> Owing to your animated exertions, and the vigorous measures of your *patrons*, you may soon hope to see the happy inhabitants of this prosperous island express but one opinion, and act with one accord, the rich and the powerful shall be tranquilly triumphant, the low and the wretched patiently submissive, great men shall eat white bread in peace, and the poor feed on barley cakes in silence. Every person in the kingdom shall acknowledge the blessings of a strong regular government; while the absurd doctrine of the Rights of Man, shall be no more thought of, or respected, than the rights of horses, asses, dogs, and dromedaries

[37] Redding, II: 322.

[38] Derek Roper, *Reviewing before the Edinburgh 1788-1802* (London: Methuen & Co., 1978), 23.

Beckford draws attention to a litany of public issues in need of redress. They include rising taxes, repressive legislation, religious intolerance, the denial of human rights, the problem of weak harvests, the threat of famine, widespread discontent in the country, general neglect of the poor, and the apathy of the rich and powerful. These liberal views were unusual for a member of the English landowner class in 1796 and seem more appropriate for William Godwin than Beckford. This republican outlook may help to explain why he chose George Robinson (1737-1801), the 'king of booksellers' to publish *Modern Novel Writing*. Robinson's firm was considered sympathetic to political radicalism and dissenting views. The senior George and his partners, in fact, were fined in 1793 for selling copies of Thomas Paine's *Rights of Man*.[39] This was the same year that he published Godwin's *An Enquiry Concerning Political Justice*. It is also significant that Helen Maria Williams turned to him in 1796 to publish the second volume of her *Letters from France*. While it would be inaccurate to classify Beckford as a political radical, he certainly held radical social views and maintained anti-establishment sentiments throughout his life.[40] The Whig tradition of his father, the popular Lord Mayor of London, undoubtedly had some measure of influence on him. Another influential figure in shaping Beckford's more liberal political and social opinions was the Earl of Chatham, William Pitt's father and prominent Whig Prime Minister of the mid-eighteenth century. The elder Pitt was Beckford's godfather and, following the death of the Lord Mayor, assumed a major role in the young Beckford's educational development, directing Beckford's political leanings towards the popular side and to the liberalism of the Whig party.

It must have seemed a significant irony to Beckford, therefore, that the son of the great Chatham would be responsible for an array of repressive measures in the 1790s, including the suspension of Habeas Corpus, the Traitorous Correspondence Act, and the Treasonable and Seditious acts of Parliament that inhibited the liberties of the people of England. Beckford and Pitt were actually childhood friends and had seen each other many times at Chatham's Burton Pynsent estate in Somerset. While their relationship seemed to start out well, an enmity developed between them as they moved into adulthood. Pitt may have experienced some resentment with how impressed his father was with Beckford's quick wit, genius and capacity for speaking—talents that the Prime Minister believed boded well for a promising political future for

---

[39] Ian Maxted, *The London Book Trades 1775-1800* (Folkestone: Dawson, 1977), 191-2.

[40] For a discussion of Beckford's radicalism, see Boyd Alexander, *England's Wealthiest Son* (London: Centaur Press, 1962), 139-51.

the Fonthill heir. The Revd John Lettice, Beckford's private tutor, confirmed
as much when he wrote that 'this illustrious Statesman was frequently heard
to exclaim with rapture at the performance of Mr. Beckford's early exercises,
particularly in oratory, and often to declare, that he saw in his childhood,
a mind more pregnant with the seeds of genius and great talents than
had almost ever occurred to him in any other instance.' On one occasion,
Chatham actually goaded his son on Beckford's performance as an orator:
'May you, my son, some day make as brilliant a speaker.'[41] Such open praise
could have sown some seeds of jealousy in the younger Pitt. Nevertheless,
the paths of Beckford and Pitt diverged as they grew older. Beckford never
became the statesman that Chatham had hoped for him to be. Instead, it
was Chatham's own son who achieved the reigns of political power at the
early age of twenty-four. Beckford's artistic temperament was ill suited for
the pragmatic world of politics, though he continued to be an astute observer
of his times and deeply concerned about the state of his country. It is clear
that he believed that Pitt in his role as a political leader had demonstrated an
abandonment of the Whig principles of his father and showed a preference
in office for 'power over principle.'[42] One of Beckford's most penetrating
observations about Pitt was when he compared him to Napoleon. Both men
he characterized as creatures of 'systems'—'wheel within wheel ... set a-going
by some invisible agency.' Neither of them, he felt, 'shared in common with
the rest of mankind those feelings which belong to flesh and blood.' Instead,
they were 'insensible as brass and iron to tears or remonstrances' until the
time came when 'sentiments more allied to Nature and humanity arose
... and Europe awoke to another state of things, wondering she had ever
submitted to such mechanical enslavement.'[43] Thus, it was these ingrained
sympathies with the struggling middle and lower classes, the influence of his
Whig background, and the view of himself as an outsider that help to explain
in large part Beckford's unorthodox political opinions at this time and his
need to retaliate against various forms of authority.

---

[41] 'William Beckford, Esq. of Fonthill,' *The European Magazine, and London Review*, 32 (September,
1797): 148. See also J. W. Oliver, *The Life of William Beckford* (London: Oxford University Press), 8.

[42] Redding, II: 219; 318.

[43] As quoted by Alexander, 259-60.

III

Although much of the satire might be lost to the reader of today, contemporary reviews of *Modern Novel Writing* were uniformly positive. The first and most substantive appeared in the *Monthly Review* in August 1796. The reviewer judged *Modern Novel Writing* to be a 'truly comic' effort, by a 'hand of a master,' a deft burlesque of the 'ordinary run of our circulating-library-novels.'[44] Revealing a strong literary background, the reviewer cited Jonathan's Swift's poem 'Love Song in the Modern Taste' (1733) as a possible inspiration for the book, an understandable identification in light of the opening lines of the poem which were very much in accord with the character of Beckford's satire: 'Fluttering spread thy purple pinions,/ Gentle Cupid o'er my heart;/ I a slave in thy dominions; Nature must give way to art.' Demonstrating, as well, awareness of the shifting trends towards the new creed of sentiment, the reviewer expressed concerns about the 'absurd incoherences of the generality of these literary mushrooms, (which so plenteously spring up every month of the year).' He described *Modern Novel Writing* as a magnifying glass that artfully displayed the novel genre diverging from its roots in 'realism' with the employment of such extravagances as 'unnatural characters, improbable incidents, ill-founded prospects of happiness, nonsensical attachments, and their distresses,' which he believed, violated common sense and outraged the 'natural order and course of things.' The review concluded with high praise for the book: 'In truth, we have, in our language, few instances in which literary mimicry, or *imitative ridicule*, has so happily produced its full effect, without the formality of censure, or the trouble of criticism.' But, the reviewer hastened to add, that the forces of change were too strong to abate through satire. To 'think of reforming the swarm of novel-writers' by this method 'would be a project more romantic, if possible, than their own romances.'

The *Monthly Mirror* followed with a somewhat less enthusiastic endorsement of the book, pointing to Charles Dodd's earlier satire, *The Curse of Sentiment* (1787) as a work that anticipated *Modern Novel Writing*. But the reviewer still considered Beckford's novel to be a 'very ingenious and successful satire on the lumber of circulating libraries.'[45] The *Critical Review* believed that 'in flights

---

[44] *The Monthly Review*, 20 (August, 1796): 477. The reviewer of this article (no. 44) was not identified by Benjamin Nangle in his book *The Monthly Review Second Series 1790-1815 Index of Contributors and Articles* (Oxford: Clarendon Press, 1955). However, the review has all of the earmarks of William Enfield (1741-1797), who was a regular contributor and considered to be a distinguished reviewer of contemporary novels and poetry for this periodical and for *The Monthly Magazine*.

[45] *The Monthly Mirror*, 2 (September, 1796): 286.

of wild and digressive humour' this book made Sterne's *Tristram Shandy* seem like a 'regular and methodical work.'[46] 'Our author seems, by his rambling, unconnected style, to intend a satire on the obscure, desultory, incorrect manner of the inferior novelists; neither do those of a higher class wholly escape the shafts of his ridicule: a variety of quotations, both in poetry and prose, many of them from writers of celebrity, are introduced, in circumstances so ludicrous, and attended with combinations so whimsical, as to render them, in their new situations, truly laughable.' Even *The British Critic*, one of the targets of Beckford's criticism, sung its praises. 'This is a very humorous and successful, though sometimes overcharged, attack upon modern novel-writing,' the reviewer wrote. He then observes: 'There is a great deal of good food for laughter in these volumes, in which we have heartily joined, though we ourselves are occasionally the subject of the writer's humour.'[47]

The early reviews of both *Modern Novel Writing* and *Azemia* did not suspect that Beckford was the author. Under the cloak of anonymity, he was free to vent his spleen against some of the literary and political extravagances of his day without fear of reprisal. In the case of *Modern Novel Writing*, reviewers readily recognized that Lady Harriet Marlow was an assumed named. *The Monthly Review* provided a footnote to its review, observing from internal evidence that 'the writer is really of the masculine gender.' They claimed the name had been 'sounded in our ears' but did not believe that they had the authority to 'report the whisper.' [48] The *Critical Review* ventured to ascribe 'this whimsical performance' to the 'pen of a gentleman well known for his poetical compositions' but provided no further identification.[49] By January 1797 *The British Critic* and *The Monthly Magazine & British Register* identified the whispered name as that of Robert Merry.[50] In its review of *Azemia*, the *Critical Review* went further by noting that 'this performance is written upon the plan of *Modern Novel Writing*' and that 'Miss J. A. M. Jenks is of the same sex with lady Harriet Marlow, *alias*, Robert Merry, esq.' [51]

While Merry, alias Della Crusca, was considered a sentimental versifier, he had also become known by this time for his vigorously pro-French and

---

[46] *Critical Review*, 18 (December, 1796): 472.

[47] *The British Critic*, 9 (January, 1797)1 75 6.

[48] *The Monthly Review*, 20: 477.

[49] *Critical Review*, 18: 472.

[50] *The British Critic*, 9: 76; *The Monthly Magazine and British Register*, 3 (January, 1797): 47.

[51] *Critical Review*, 20 (August, 1797): 470.

anti-Pitt views, which may explain why he was identified as the author. The misattribution may also have something to do with the strong criticism of William Gifford in *Modern Novel Writing*. The assault on Gifford in both books may have been perceived by contemporaries as Merry's method of seeking revenge. Ironically, the reviewers failed to see Merry himself as an object of attack in the thrusts against the sentimentality of Della Cruscan verse in *Azemia*.

Beckford was able to keep his authorship of these two novels a secret for over twenty years before he divulged the truth to Samuel Rogers and then confirmed it later with Britton and Cyrus Redding. It was necessary to do so in view of the risks one had to face at this time for publicly criticizing the government and its leaders. While these writings were borne out of Beckford's own feelings of social and political isolation, there is, beneath the surface of *Modern Novel Writing* and *Azemia*, a display of incisive social and political criticism that contributes to their historical significance and that calls for a renewed critical assessment of these neglected works.[52] In Beckford's mind the form of sentimentalism promoted by such writers as Samuel Richardson, Henry Fielding, and Laurence Sterne had now become the province of second- and third-rate novelists. Furthermore, these new sentimental novels were being aided near the end of the century by the proliferation of circulating libraries. Beckford feared that by making such inferior literary works available, the circulating libraries were fostering a taste for them. Particularly troublesome to him was that the sentimental view of reality seemed an absurd defense against the harsh realities of war, poverty, and political oppression in the 1790s. Sensibility carried to such extremes seemed grotesquely escapist at a time when more realism and common sense were needed. And it is on this point that the political and sentimental satire of these two novels converge and achieve a coherent thematic relationship. For Beckford, circulating-library novels of the sentimental strain provided a vision of life that was equivalent to the political schemes of Pitt's government—both were equally irrational and irresponsible in view of the serious social and political challenges that England was facing at this time.

ROBERT J. GEMMETT
Spencerport, N. Y.

---

[52] A separate critical edition of *Azemia* is in preparation and will be published as a companion volume following the publication of this edition.

𝕸𝖔𝖉𝖊𝖗𝖓 𝕹𝖔𝖛𝖊𝖑 𝕮𝖚𝖗𝖎𝖙𝖎𝖓𝖌,

OR THE

ELEGANT ENTHUSIAST;

AND

Interefting Emotions

OF

Arabella Bloomville.

A RHAPSODICAL ROMANCE;

INTERSPERSED WITH

𝕻𝖔𝖊𝖙𝖗𝖞,

IN TWO VOLUMES.

𝖁𝖔𝖑. 1.

BY THE RIGHT HON.

LADY HARRIET MARLOW.

I nod in company, I wake at night,
Fools rush into my head, and fo I write.

Pope.

𝕷𝖔𝖓𝖉𝖔𝖓 :

PRINTED FOR G. G. AND J. ROBINSON,

MDCCXCVI.

Title-page of Beckford's personal copy of *Modern Novel Writing*, 1796
Courtesy of the Beinecke Library, Yale University.

A detail from James Gillray's 'New Morality', 1798
Courtesy of Lewis Walpole Library, Yale University.

MODERN NOVEL WRITING, OR THE ELEGANT ENTHUSIAST

VOLUME I

To her Grace the Duchess of _____,

Madam,

Athough the captivating diffidence of your Grace's noble mind forbids me to prefix your name to this dedication, yet when I affirm that to all the exterior charms of person, and a loveliness beyond compare, you add the most engaging and condescending manners, joined to the extreme of every human virtue, it will be impossible that you should remain concealed:---no, Madam, the observant and adoring public will instantly discover my enchanting Friend and Patroness, whose greatness of soul cannot brook even the idea of flattery, but whose characteristic it is to

Do good by stealth, and blush to find it fame.[1]

As it has been entirely owing to the fostering smiles of your Grace's approbation that this little work presumes to shew itself to the world, so I am emboldened to hope that the enlightened reader will not find it totally destitute of merit. I have, indeed, endeavoured to unite correct, delicate, and vivid imagery to an animated moral sensibility, and at the same time to enrich it by various incident, lively sallies, fashionable intrigue, picturesque description, and, in fine, to mark it with the striking features of a bold originality, without which, no daughter of the Muses can ever expect to produce that phoenix of literary zoology—a perfect novel.

I have the honor and happiness to be,
Madam,
Your Grace's most obliged,
Most obedient, most devoted
And most affectionate humble servant.
Harriet Marlow

Hyacinth Lodge,
March 31, 1796.

---

[1] Alexander Pope, *Epilogue to the Satires*, Dialogue I, l. 136.

I

A Rural Picture

At the foot of a verdant declivity overshadowed by woodbine, jessamine and myrtle, and softly inundated by a sapphire rivulet that wandered through the neighbouring woods in serpentine simplicity, stood the sweet and elegant retired cottage of Arabella Bloomville. A majestic grove of aged oaks nodded in awful and sublime splendor on one side, while abrupt and fantastic rocks added dignity to the scene on the other. Here in spring was heard the mellifluous chorus of the goldfinch, the throstle, the linnet, the blackbird, the cuckoo, and the woodlark, nor was the melancholy bird of evening silent when the sun hid himself behind the western horizon. It was then that the pensive and matchless Arabella indulged her tender grief, and softly answered with her sighs to the pathetic melody of the feathered songstress. O enviable state of retired competence, how widely different from the turbulent occupations of exalted life, where vanity and factitious joys corrode the heart, and robbing it of its native captivation, leave us nothing but a blank!

Here the lovely girl would sit for hours with her blushing cheek pressed upon her lily hand, ruminating on the various disasters of her undirected youth, so young, and so unhappy! and here also the cherished miniature of her beloved absent Henry would prey upon her feelings.

> She sat, like patience on a monument
> Smiling at grief.[2]

Her dear and valuable parents in the grave, alas! the amiable orphan thus left to her own sad reflection in the very blossom of her days, without a friend into whose bosom she could pour her desolating woe; except the faithful Margaret Grimes, who had been the companion of her earliest infancy, and who had attended her through every vicissitude of her uncommon destiny. Arabella was but in the first spring of life, seventeen summers only had bleached her

---

[2] Shakespeare. [Beckford's note]. *Twelfth Night*, II, iv, ll. 117-18

snowy bosom, yet the fatal experience of evil had more than doubled her years; what breast but must sympathize with such suffering excellence?

> Let those feel now, who never felt before,
> Let those who always felt, now feel the more.[3]

Here for a moment let us drop the veil of oblivion on so deeply interesting a contemplation.

---

[3] Appears to be Thomas Parnell's translation of lines originally from *Pervigilium Veneris*, sometimes ascribed to Catullus. The original lines are: *Cras amet qui numquam amavit;/ Quique amavit, cras amet* ('Let him love tomorrow who never loved before; and he as well who has loved, let him love tomorrow'). Parnell's version reads: 'Let those love now who never loved before;/Let those who always loved, now love the more.' John Bartlett, *Familiar Quotations* (Boston, 1919), no. 3219.

II

A Storm at Sea

Henry Lambert, was the only son of Colonel and Lady Maria Lambert, his Father had sat several sessions in the British Parliament with the most exemplary and noble incorruptibility. Now though a rich grandmother on the maternal side was but just returned from Canada when the Newmarket races began, yet the ancient country seat had been completely repaired upon the occasion, and the captivating diversion of the chase frequently afforded them the happiest relaxation.

Henry was now in the twenty-fourth year of his age, and had already served three campaigns with unsuspected honor, when it so fell out, that the ship meeting with a most tremendous gale on the coast of Guinea about two months after his first journey to Madrid, the finer feelings of the celestial Arabella suffered a new and more terrible shock, which the lenient hand of time could alone hope to mollify. The original breaking of his collar bone, by the fall from his famous hunter, which had once so cruelly alarmed the ladies in the park, was no longer an object of material magnitude, but the execrable idea of those barbarous savages, and the innumerable difficulties he might labor under, was indeed a stroke which required the utmost fortitude, and every religious consideration to combat and sustain. Neither the Colonel, nor Lady Maria, nor even the languishing Arabella herself had received any intelligence for many weeks, so that his gout not returning at its accustomed period, the old couple repaired to Bath, where a great number of distinguished foreigners were already assembled.

The house however they had hired on the forest was so completely out of repair, that the distant bells from the village had a peculiar pathos, when the benighted traveller reposed himself in the hawthorn grove. This could not be prevented, by the usual operation of foresight, nor did the howling of the yard dog, during the tempest, in any manner decrease the general perturbation. Lady Maria indeed who slept in the attic story first caught the alarm, and rushing through the flames, descended by a back staircase into the garden. The clock struck ONE at the moment, and the awful solemnity of the scene was horribly impressive. Yet but a little while before she might have collected herself with propriety, even though the danger had been ten times more imminent, for in all active emergency, nature is prone to subside, and yield the palm to the consistency of power. The expected visitors not coming the next day, rendered the situation of Lady Maria still more perplexing, because she had promised the Duchess and the Miss Pebleys to meet them at the rooms that very evening.

There is no rank in life exempt from misfortunes, and even the happiest of mortals have but too much reason to complain: from his internal resources Man can alone hope to triumph in the hour of trial.

Well, all intercourse for the time was necessarily broken off, and Arabella's picture, painted by the immortal West,[4] which hung in the grand saloon, having suffered the most material injury, it was thought adviseable to wait the result of their last dispatches, and not further improve the grounds till the ensuing spring; for as the Colonel was far advanced in years, and Henry's taste had not been consulted in the affair, it was difficult to ascertain how long it might be before the wished-for union of the young people could take place. This reflection too often embittered the vernal hours of the blooming Arabella, and thus impressed with melancholy ideas, her active mind would frequently call aid from the tender muse to dissipate her chagrin. The following sweet lines may give a specimen of her exquisite poetical powers.

Sonnet

When sorrow's humblest haunts reflect the beam
  That patient virtue scatters o'er the plain,
No wanton zephyr curls the languid stream,
  No melting woodlark wakes the warbled strain.

For me, alas! beset with storms of woe,
  Where plaintive ecchoes die upon the gale,
May the still voice of agony bestow,
  The softest requiem to the rustic vale.

O! my lov'd Henry! shouldst thou ever hear
  How feebly flows the meditated lay,

---

[4] Benjamin West (1738-1820), President of the Royal Academy, and prominent Anglo-American painter of historical and religious subjects. Beckford developed a close association with West and was sufficiently impressed with his work to commission seventeen paintings for Fonthill Abbey that was under construction around the time *Modern Novel Writing* was published.

While the pale moonshine gilds the checquer'd sphere;
Thou might'st again the distant theme display,

Might'st drop th' appropriate plaudit of a tear,
And whisper sweetness to the charms of May.

By amusements such as these, would the divine Arabella beguile the threatning difficulties, for the youthful mind is almost always amiable, while hoary time hardens the heart, alas! too often with the muscular anatomy. As there was great reason to suppose that the system of ethics they had strenuously adopted was in fact defective, so, Lady Maria, by the advice of the Duchess, prevailed upon the Colonel to leave London without loss of time, for no vessel could arrive after the monsoons were set in. Having passed a week in their passage with Sir George Darlington, and gone through the vexatious ceremony of a regular presentation, they fortunately arrived at the asylum of their hopes, when the fragrant dews of evening were on every side arising from the surrounding lakes.

III

A Terrible Encounter

During the siege, Henry Lambert particularly distinguished himself by that prevailing suavity which operates beyond the shafts of courage, or even the prevalence of despair. Now the commanding Officer's horse having been killed under him, the whole plan of the attack was immediately changed, and indeed it became every hour more necessary, for vegetables were uncommonly scarce, and what was still worse, no letters had arrived from England. It was therefore properly decided by the military council, that the theatres should be closed during the remainder of the week; nor need this be much wondered at, for the commonest candles were three and sixpence each, and there really was not a single wheelwright to be found in the whole vicinity.

Henry, therefore, whose mind was half distracted by a variety of occurrences, leaped hastily into his phaeton and four, and pursued his journey with the highest animation. The Old Woman, whose early influence might have demanded a more permanent attention in the present instance, had conjured him to stay, with tears in her eyes, but his military duty got the better of all selfish considerations, while the fond remembrance of his adorable Arabella pressed closely to his heart, and occupied all his senses.

The moon now scattered her virgin tints over an unclouded hemisphere, when he reached the sea shore, but the baggage wagon had been gone above an hour, and as the mountain was inaccessible in consequence of the immense fall of snow, he determined to postpone his project till the morrow, when he might look for the arrival of his friends Fergusson, and Jennings to assist him in the undertaking.

It was not however easy under such circumstances, to approach the farm house, for the walls were covered with ivy, and many of the elms had been blown down at the preceding assizes; besides, the Bishop and Sir George Walker had absolutely forbidden any person to kill game in that neighbourhood. The gallant Henry was entirely at a loss what to do in so critical an emergency, when calling to mind his early attachment, and subsequent promise to the divine Arabella, at the same time recollecting all the disasters he had suffered on her account, he heaved a gentle but heart-rending sigh, and beckoning to his servant, who was half petrified with fear, hastily seized his pistols.

The Bear was within ten yards of him, when the shot missed, so that if his foot had not struck against the jutting root of an old oak which in some degree broke his fall, he, in all probability would have perished. There was now no alternative, for the shepherd's boy who had been present at the outset of the conflict, was unable to get round the garden in time, and the ice suddenly gave way, therefore had not Henry at the same moment sprung forward, with the utmost activity, the Bear must inevitably have escaped.

The farmer, whose gratitude knew no bounds for the signal service which Henry had thus rendered him, entreated the young soldier to partake of his frugal board, and the beautiful Marianne who gazed upon him with ineffable delight, added infinitely to his delicate embarrassment. Now it happened that an owl had destroyed all the pigeons, and there was no market on a Saturday, notwithstanding which, Henry slept more serenely on his humble pallet, than perhaps the most luxurious nobleman on his bed of down. The visionary image of his celestial Arabella enriched his slumbers with fancy's fairy train. O! had the mistress of his soul been witness to all those mental agitations, which originate in true love, yet which her own tender sensations had sufficiently inculcated, the restless doubts that harass the subjugated spirit, would have given way to the most unbounded confidence; but the real event of things is never known till, perhaps, the remedy is inapplicable, as Mr. Chapman would often tell Henry in their moments of relaxation. But then the latter seldom failed to exclaim—'You cannot conceive the perfection of my Arabella, she is the Paphian queen in all her glory.'

> Grace is in all her steps, Heav'n in her eye,
> In all her gestures dignity and love.[5]

---

[5] Milton. [Beckford's note]. *Paradise Lost*, Bk VIII, ll. 488-9.

IV

A Polite Circle

The sudden appearance of the Bear had produced great anxiety in the minds of the three women in the cart, but the Curate was by no means to blame, for he had not been a fishing before for six months, and was totally ignorant of the matter. Lord Giblet had indeed promised him a pointer if the parliament should be dissolved before the frost set in, but the light dragoons who were quartered in the next village, had absolutely sold their library by public auction. This naturally occasioned much deep investigation, in the polite circle which the Colonel and Lady Maria Lambert joined, at the magnificent castle of Sir George Darlington. This castle was situated on a rising eminence, with a beautiful command of the adjacent prospect, where verdant meadows and fallow lands, upon either bank of a rapid navigable river delighted the roving eye. Cattle of every kind there cropped their green delicious banquet, and there the placid sheep by their innocent bleatings gently aroused the plaintive ecchoes of the circumambient groves. 'My charming Lucinda,' said the Countess of Fairville, as she lightly took up a bit of muffin with her taper fingers, 'My dear girl I fear there is some latent cause that preys upon your vernal prime, and casts this fatal gloom over your naturally gay spirits.' A lucid drop quivered upon the eyelid of Lucinda, she could not speak, but letting fall her teacup upon the floor, tenderly exclaimed, 'O madam, your ladyship's attention and affecting kindness oppress me still more than even the severity of my fate, alas! your ladyship is too good, indeed you are all perfection.' Having uttered these words, she fainted, but Miss Perkins running with a bottle of salts, and Dr. Philbert softly chafing her temples, she by degrees recovered her wonted serenity of aspect, and cast a languishing look of pathetic meaning towards the Countess, whose charming cheeks were already bathed in tears. To the amazement of all present, at this instant, upstarted Lord Mahogany, and with a frown declared, that the prevalence of sedition was become abominable, especially in this happy country where the poor are equally protected with the rich, and which enjoys the most perfect constitution that the wisdom of man could invent, which is as incorruptible in its principle as generally beneficial in its practice. Having uttered this with an indignant tone of rage, he overturned the silver tea urn on

Lucy Melville's favorite lapdog, which Major Pemberton had brought her from the East Indies, and to which she was attached with perhaps an improper, yet enthusiastic fondness.

The maid servant who had been sent up stairs for the *Castle of Otranto*,[6] met Matthew the butler on the landing place, and being in the secret of Lucinda's perturbation, asked him rather petulantly, whether Jim the groom had sent the parson the potatoes. As lady Di Martin came out of the parlour, she eagerly enquired if the Letters were come in, which very much tended to confirm Matthew's suspicion, for as Captain Warley and his three sisters were expected to dinner, it gave a scope to the discussion. In the mean time Lord Mahogany, though one of the best chess players in Europe could not find his *spencer*, and as the key of the hall door had been left in the green-house, by Peggy Tomlinson the housemaid, so it was absolutely impossible to get the chaise ready in time. The confusion therefore was great in every part of that venerable mansion, yet the hapless Lucinda, profiting of the occasion, suffered herself to be led quietly to her chamber by the compassionating Countess; then throwing herself upon a chintz sopha she gave vent to the most lamentable accents of anguish and despair. Had the sentinel kept his word, perhaps nothing of the kind would have happened, for Lord Mahogany's first wife was a cheesemonger's daughter, and his eldest child had been born with a hare lip; this therefore was the only circumstance that could so materially have offended him. A vindictive mind, it must be owned, is a scourge to the possessor, for one of the greatest virtues is, that a man should learn to subdue his passions.

At dinner the Earl gave way to his usual merriment, and rallied Sukey Sanders upon her mistaken attachment, but unfortunately the venison was over roasted, and the youngest Miss Warley having swallowed a pin, Henry's letter which that moment arrived, was thrown into the fire by mistake. Now as the Mayor's ball had been the night before, and as the High Sheriff was gone to London, so the absence of Colonel Lambert and his Lady was doubly unfortunate.

How to remedy this inconvenience occupied the thoughts of Lord Mahogany during the whole night, though he had sent to Arabella but the week before, for a pot of tamarinds, and who, but for this fatal catastrophe, might have gained some intelligence of her valuable and beloved Henry. But alas! in the present instance, poor Margaret Grimes was obliged to return home without the shadow of a consolation, and to acquaint her agitated lady, that her every hope was abortive in the extreme.

---

[6] A new London edition of Horace Walpole's *Castle of Otranto* was published by Cooper and Graham in 1796.

V

Description of a Beauty

Arabella, as has been observed, had now attained her seventeenth year: her form was the animated portrait of her mind; truth, benignity, pure and unstudied delicacy, the meekness of sensibility, and the dignity of innate virtue, claimed the esteem, while the exquisite beauty of her bewitching countenance captivated the heart of every beholder![7] She was tall, and finely proportioned; her complexion was neither the insipid whiteness of the lily-bosomed Circassian, nor the masculine shade of the Gallic brunette; the freshness of health glowed upon her cheek, while the lustre of her dark blue eyes borrowed its splendor from the unsullied flame, that gave her mind the perfection of intellect! Her hair which fell over her shoulders in copious ringlets, was of the most beautiful brown, rather inclining to the auburn, and her teeth and lips,

Were pearls within a ruby case.

Her bosom was the throne of love, full, firm, and fairer than the purest ivory; her voice was mild as the cooings of the ring-dove; and her smile the gentle harbinger of tenderness and complacency! She had also acquired considerable eminence in the science of harmony: her singing was the seraphic eccho of her lute, whose chords spoke to the soul, under the magic touch of her skilful fingers. She had all that animation which is more usually found among the natives of the South of Europe; yet this spirited expression often melted into softness so insinuating, that it was difficult to say whether pensive tenderness

---

[7] The description of Arabella here derives from Mary Robinson's *Vancenza; or, The Dangers of Credulity* (London, 1792), I: 17-18. Source identified by Deborah Griebel, 'A Critical Edition of William Beckford's *Modern Novel Writing* and *Azemia*,' Ph.D. dissertation (University of Toronto, 1984), 381. Robinson's novel enjoyed enormous popularity with the entire print run selling out on the first day of publication. Paula Byrne, Robinson's biographer, highlights the elements of the novel that explain why it was an easy prey for Beckford's satire: 'The novel as a whole is a typical "romance," with improbable plot lines, elaborate poetical language ("novel slang," as Austen called it), and clichéd heroines and heroes.' See *Perdita The Literary, Theatrical, Scandalous Life of Mary Robinson* (New York: Random House), 275.

or sparkling vivacity was the most predominant: in short she was every thing that fancy could picture or conviction adore! Perfection could go no further. Her arms were of a delicate snowy whiteness, and cast in the most exquisite mould of tapering formation, and her little feet were so enchantingly pretty, that they ravished all beholders. Such was Arabella.

Henry Lambert, the dear object of her unalterable affections, was equally engaging in his person for a man, as she was for a female. He was six feet two inches in height, and his form was the most elegant that can be conceived, but his face surpassed all description, such sensibility marked every feature! his eyes sparkling with native vivacity, were of a bright hazle, his nose was inclined to the Grecian, he had the most beautiful mouth and teeth ever beheld, with uncommonly fine dark hair, and beautifully spreading whiskers, the whole heightened by a complexion fair as alabaster;

Ah! sure a pair was never seen,
 So justly form'd to meet, by nature,
The youth excelling so in mien,
 The maid in ev'ry grace of feature.[8]

---

[8] These are lines from the first stanza of a song presented by Don Carlos in Richard Brinsley Sheridan's *Duenna*, II, ii.

VI

Fresh Embarrassments

Fate seemed to have interwove in the same loom the destinies of Arabella Bloomville and Lucinda Howard, and the touching sensibilities were equally appropriate to either. The wanderings of fancy and the ebullitions of the imagination may indeed awhile mislead the most amiable, but consistent virtue can neither be shaken nor controuled. The gay flowers of hope cannot long stem the current of adversity, which, in its rapid endeavours spreads a dragon wing over every ray of human comfort. Arabella thus separated from her Lucinda, had no resource but in the soothing melodies of her piano forte, on which she played with bewitching delicacy,

> Her flying fingers touch'd the keys,
> And heavenly joys inspired.[9]

Nor did the worthy Mr. Bangrove, curate of the little flock amongst which she lived, ever deviate from those principles which reconcile us to the losses of this life, and lead us through a dreary wilderness of earthly turmoil, to a flowery paradise of hope.

It was in one of those delicious nights, when the heavens are bespangled with stars, and tranquil silence sits brooding over the autumnal plain, that Sir Peter Sampson's elegant gig drove by her open window; the lonely owl sung a horrid dirge to the murmuring stream that meandered by the side of the road over which it passed, though the worthy Baronet himself seemed deeply absorbed in the propriety of a general inclosure of waste lands. Now Margaret Grimes, having but just gathered the mistletoe, could not give the wondering Arabella any further means of unravelling the clue, for the patient villagers were for the most part retired to their placid rest, and unfortunately the mail coach had neither brought the oysters, nor the French dictionary.

---

[9] John Dryden, 'Alexander's Feast or, the Power of Music; An Ode in Honor of St. Ceclia's Day,' II, ll. 22-4: 'With flying fingers touch'd the lyre:/ The trembling notes ascend the sky,/ And heav'nly joys inspire.'

This occasioned a more material embarrassment, and threw a new light upon the subject, for if Lieutenant Jenkinson had really quitted his lodgings in Dover Street, and the muslins had not arrived, it was absolutely impossible for either of them by the utmost stretch of their ingenuity to solve the enigma. It was certain that the county justices had dined together the preceding Friday, and that the militia was speedily to be embodied; but in the interim the right wing of the old mansion might be taken down, and the prospect from the high ground rendered much more interesting: now in that case it must be difficult for the beauteous Arabella to divine how far her fondest wishes could expect ever to be realized. Under this impression of suspence and anxiety, Arabella flew for refuge to her harp, which had the power of consolation in all emergencies. She then sweetly sung the following delicious air, accompanied by the silver melody of the instrument:

Song

Love is a soft, involuntary flame,
　　Beyond the pow'r of language to express;
That throws resistless magic o'er the frame,
　　And leads to boundless pleasure or distress.

From love misfortune takes her earliest date,
　　Or rapt'rous bliss prepares the flow'ry way;
Wak'd at our birth, they mingle with our fate,
　　And cling to life, till vanquish'd by decay.

E'en when in youth we feel the hand of death
　　Obscure the prospect of a cloudless sky.
All conqu'ring love attends the fleeting breath,
　　And Nature's fond, last effort, is a sigh.

Then tell me. Henry! what avail the cares
　　That taint our joys with bitterness and pain?
If to our aid the god of love repairs,
　　And Henry smiles, misfortunes frown in vain.

Having finished her song, she wiped a crystal tear from her glittering eye, and again betook herself to reflection. Persons, alas! can easily judge the conduct of others, where themselves are not compromised, but to preserve the true medium under every disadvantage, is, and must ever be, a most difficult endeavour. Not but that there are distinguished personages in high life who draw different conclusions, and form their mode of conduct on a more extensive system: but the greatest allowance must surely be made for an unfortunate young woman launched into life without a compass or a guide. Nothing peculiarly interesting happened the succeeding day, but about eleven at night, the belfry took fire, and nobody could pass the ferry on account of Mrs. Pendigrass's lying in, for the London Doctor had gone by mistake to Banbury, and bought all the best pictures before Lord Damplin's agent could get there.

The hunting season being now pretty generally at an end, except upon the lakes, which were innavigable, and amongst the smaller hamlets, so the best part of Sir George Mumford's grounds were entirely overflowed. The gardiner certainly was not to blame in the affair, for his wife had absolutely consented to the marriage of her youngest daughter, and had the carpenter himself acted an honourable part, every article might have been happily arranged; but Miss Sanders's intrigue coming to light at the very moment, not a human being in the neighbourhood thought proper to interfere. In consequence of this succession of untoward circumstances, the probability of Henry's speedy return was fainter than heretofore, and the charming Arabella found no longer any comfort in tending her little family of flowers, but renouncing every species of active amusement, entirely devoted herself to the study of the *Belles Lettres*. In this, by degrees she succeeded wonderfully, and gave some light productions to the public, that discovered an animated genius and a liberal mind, and being totally free from vanity, prejudice or affectation, were particularly admired by the celebrated Miss Maria Helen,[10] who is so justly celebrated throughout Europe for the impartiality of her writings, and her *rational* love of liberty. As for the melancholy Arabella she embraced the only opportunity that offered itself to obtain a momentary tranquility, or occasionally to dissipate her chagrin.

---

[10] Helen Maria Williams (1762-1827), poet, novelist and letter writer, was an unshakeable advocate of the French Revolution and its ideals, to which Beckford ironically alludes, and well-known for her *Letters Written from France in the Summer of 1790*, with continuing instalments in 1792, 1795, and 1796.

VII

The Discovery of a Stranger

General Barton had a noble mansion at but a little distance from the humble abode of the mellifluous Arabella: and being rather of a choleric disposition, would oftentimes indulge himself in a free use of wine. As he was an excellent player at billiards, and had in the early part of life visited most of the courts upon the Continent, he could never be brought to adopt the fashionable mode of improving his extensive premises. Not however being particularly fond of field sports, but in fact almost a martyr to a violent bilious disorder, his house was constantly frequented by a number of rakish companions. As sitting pensively under a weeping willow by the side of a purling stream was a favorite occupation of the amiable Lucinda Howard as well as of Arabella, so General Barton would sometimes saunter in the hayfields during the Turtle season, and amuse himself by singing the following lively air, which had in consequence become extremely popular in the country:

Air

Ye Gods disperse
This painful verse,
By some wild whirlwind thro' the skies!
Lest in amaze-
Ment at my lays,
The folks my folly should despise.

Then chip the bread, and lay the cloth,
Nor will we differ while we dine;
Dear Phillis! I have got some broth,
Some parsley, bacon, beans, and wine.

Nay start not, sweet maiden! at what I require,
The gridiron is hissing e'en now on the fire,

>And whatever you fancy for filling your belly,
>You shall have, tho' a Griffin, in savory jelly.

The General indeed did not so much indulge his comic vein in this manner, with a view to promote his interest in the county, as to learn what merchants settled in that quarter were most famous for their breed of horses. Now had he but possessed a mule of his own, or had lived in any intimacy with a biscuit baker, he would probably have escaped many inconveniencies, to which his natural impetuosity rendered him liable. Be this as it may, Arabella absolutely despaired of ever again seeing her Henry, whom she was now but too fatally convinced that she loved with an ardent and unalterable affection. And surely he well merited this faithful testimony at her hands, for it must be owned, that the arrows of true passion, when sharpened by the sceptre of disappointment, envelope the heart with a weight of woe, and forcibly obumbrate the finest feelings of the soul. Animated by these observations which flowed naturally from her peculiarly interesting situation, Arabella wandered beyond the usual boundaries of her little domain, till near a small copse of Aspen and Poplar trees, she met at the close of day a most strikingly beauteous Lady, who seemed a victim to the utmost desolation and despair, and who soon made the melting Arabella forget her own proper sorrows in the tenderer emotions of a sympathetic nervous sensibility. As she gazed on the melancholy Lady, she was charmed by hearing her sing in a pathetic tone the subsequent fascinating sonnet,

>O gentle gale! could I thy flight arrest,
>   Thou soft companion of the midnight hour!
>I'd bid thee cheer with thy refreshing pow'r,
>   My absent love, and die upon his breast.
>
>Sweet plaintive bird that now forsak'st thy nest!
>   Mild Queen of Night that now aloft dost tow'r!
>His be the song, and his the moonlight bow'r,
>   No more, alas! can I with those be blest.
>
>Ah! once-loved objects which to joy invite!
>   For me you shed your soothing charms in vain,
>While that fine form no more enchants my sight,
>   My lyre I tune, but mournful is the strain:
>All that to other breasts imparts delight
>   Can only bring to me increase of pain!

As the fair stranger closed her melody, the village clock struck nine, and the solitary bat began his vespers; Arabella therefore flew to her assistance, and though Margaret Grimes had scarcely time to put on a silk gown, before the Constable had actually apprehended three poachers, and discovered Betsy Blanket and her Sweet-heart in the lane, yet Arabella seizing time by the forelock, led her new acquaintance to the woodbine bower, which amorous innocence had wove for contemplation and repose.

The London waggon had but just gone by, and the accustomed formalities passed between this exquisite pair of enchanting beauties, when Arabella prepared to listen with an engaging and compassionate attention to the sweet Lady's narrative, who, animated by the generous pity of her friend, took out a red Morocco pocket book, filled with vine leaves and violets; then collecting all her fortitude, and throwing away her inkhorn, she began as follows in the next chapter.

VIII

The Fair Stranger's Story

'My father was the youngest son of Lord Danton an Irish Baron, and happening to fall in love with the only daughter of Viscount Rosebud, he married her against the inclination of the friends of both parties. As Lucy my valuable mother was in consequence rejected by her family, and as my father's pecuniary resources were at a low ebb, so they thought it adviseable to retire to Lisbon with the little modicum they could now call their own. There my honoured father entered into the wine trade, but meeting with considerable losses in business, he died in less than four years of a broken heart, leaving his disconsolate widow, with the little Amelia, which is myself, the only remaining pledge of their affection. My excellent mamma now formed a plan of life conformable to her narrow circumstances, devoting all her time to my education, and to the improvement of my personal charms. The numberless flatterers with whom my inexperienced youth was surrounded, have told me that she succeeded in both endeavours even beyond her most ardent expectations.

'However this might have been, I grew taller and more blooming every day, till the fame of my beauty excited the attention of the principal nobility at Lisbon. I speak only of the male part, for it must be owned our sex is very envious, and the Portuguese ladies do certainly not afford an exception to the general rule.

'Don Pedro de Gonzales, a young Spanish grandee of the first class, and who was as estimable for the virtues of his heart, as he was distinguished by the incomparable elegance of his person, soon professed himself my most vehement adorer. His residence at Lisbon being at the hotel of a Dutch merchant, Mynheer Van Woolengen, which was near our habitation, and as the said merchant had married an English lady at the Brazils, Don Pedro had but too frequent opportunities to plead his tender pain to me; I, who was young, lively, handsome, animated and ingenuous, being then only in my sixteenth year, listened perhaps too willingly to his amorous tale, but on such occasions, surely a proper investigation of causes and effects might tend to do away those harsh impressions which malice, and hard-heartedness too readily imbibe.

'Now there was a Duchess de Guides who had contracted a close intimacy
with my mamma, and who had been married much against her inclination
to a man old enough to be her grandfather. The Duchess had a daughter
Adeline de Guides, whom she cherished with true maternal care, but whose
disposition was rather too violent, and indeed I may say ferocious.

'This young lady had been brought up in a convent, and was, as you may
suppose, completely bigotted to the ignorant superstition of her country, yet
having encouraged a fatal passion for the young Count Velasquez, who was
also amongst the number of my lovers, it gave birth to many cruel dangers
which afterwards threatened me, as you will see by the sequel.

'Don Pedro had formed a strict friendship with the Baron de Plombal, who,
you must know, was a near relation of Count Velasquez, had resided in England
for several years, and spoke the language of the country in its greatest purity.
He had also much distinguished himself in the Republic of Letters. I should
however previously have mentioned, that an English woman of distinction,
Lady Anna Maria Delville arrived at Lisbon from Falmouth, after a very
bad passage of fourteen days. Her ladyship had been sent thither by order of
the faculty, as her malady was supposed to be a decline or rather a galloping
consumption. In the same packet that brought her ladyship, came Captain
O'Donnel, an Irish officer, of most extraordinary beauty, and whose mind
was eminently honourable and enlightened, He had distinguished himself in
several duels by his bravery and moderation, which very much interested us all
in his favor, for we women, you know my dear madam, are always strenuous
admirers of courage in a man; nor is this to be wondered at when we consider
that woman, being the weaker vessel, stands in need of protection.

'It should seem, by the bye, that Captain O'Donnel's mother had been
a Portuguese a lady of some rank, on which account the charming fellow
found no difficulty in introducing himself to the Marquis de Suza, a minister
of state, and who was his distant relation. All the best company of Lisbon
resorted to the house of this Marquis, and amongst other persons of high
fashion, the much admired Donna Isabella Cordova, a young widow of
infinite attraction, but rather more famed for her gallantries than either for
her virtue or benevolence.

'But I should have told you beforehand, that for sometime past my dear
mother's health had been very precarious, and seemed to threaten her with
approaching dissolution, so that she determined at all events to return home
to her native land, that she might resign her existence amongst the few friends,
of whom the withering blasts of adversity had not totally deprived her.'

As the fair Stranger now perceived Arabella's liquid sorrows to flow apace
down her lovely cheeks, she paused—and as the evening mists were rolling

gradually over the side of the neighbouring hills, and thick damps were arising from the adjoining lake, Arabella led her melancholy associate to her neat but humble cottage, where the attentive Margaret Grimes soon presented them with toast and butter, eggs, tea, cake, and other elegant refreshments.

IX

Continuation of the Fair Stranger's Story

When the two ladies had finished their temperate repast, the unfortunate Amelia thus proceeded: 'I informed you, Madam, that my only parent was from sickness gradually descending to the tomb, and that in consequence we were hastening our departure from Lisbon. This fatal conjuncture, which in all probability, would separate me for ever from the sole master of my heart, the excellent Don Pedro, overwhelmed him also with despair, and forced us to adopt the rash measure of a private marriage. You must know that one of Don Pedro's family was a Benedictine Friar, and resided in a convent at a small distance from the metropolis, in perhaps one of the most delirious situations upon earth, for it stood immediately upon the banks of the Tagus. The name of this venerable Monk, was Father Laurence, yet he had in the spring of life been an officer of established bravery, and was now equally celebrated for meek resignation and unaffected piety. The superior however of this religious society, it must be observed, was an inquisitor of the holy office, and generally reputed a man of a most sanguinary disposition. I should not have touched upon his character, but that he had a nephew who was a major in the Portuguese service, who had travelled into China a few years before, and had since married a Spanish Lady, who was desperately in love with my Don Pedro. Now Don Pedro was himself of a frank and open nature, but rather too apt to place confidence in such persons as, under the hypocritical veil of sanctity, hide vices of a scarlet dye. Suffice it to say, that the nuptial ceremony was performed in the chapel belonging to the aforementioned convent, in presence of Mrs. Jemina Johnson an English shopkeeper, Mr. George Adamson, cornfactor, and Don Lopez de Ximenes. I cannot here pass over a circumstance of the most extraordinary import, for about two hours after the ceremony was performed, and I had returned home to my mother, to prevent whose suspicions, I was forced to trump up some story or other, which I have now forgot; it so happened that a famous English physician, a Doctor Lambton, arrived in the city, and had brought with him the most beautiful Newfoundland dog that ever I set eyes on in the whole course of my life. This worthy man hearing of my mother's ill state of health, thought it in some degree his duty to pay a visit to her, and offer her his advice. Now he was a very gross fat man in his person, and had a way of squinting which rendered him highly ridiculous in my eyes, so that I had much difficulty to keep my countenance while he was present, notwithstanding the perplexing predicament in which I stood. It came out from some part of his conversation that he was a Cheshire man, and an intimate friend of Sir Simon Delves, with whom my poor father had fought a duel in his early youth. The particulars my beloved mamma did not think proper to explain, though I have since discovered that a Lord Newton had been the chief instigator of the affair. But not to digress, or trespass, my dear Madam, upon your patience, the next morning at six o'clock, and without my having had any previous notice, we embarked on board the Minerva packet, Captain Peter Smith, and sailed with a fair wind for Falmouth.

'I had only been able to see my adored Don Pedro for five minutes, since we were united at the altar; but you may judge from the following verses which he slipped into my hand at our last interview, how cruel and heart-rending were the pangs of our separation. The lines were originally written in Spanish, but I have translated them at my leisure, being perfect mistress of that enchanting language.'

Verses Written by Don Pedro

How soft are the notes of the spring!
    What fragrance exhales from the grove!
Ye birds, taught by you, I would sing,
    And here I for ever could rove.

Tho' its bottom is clear, yet the rill
    Delights from the rock to descend;
So I, from Ambition's steep hill,
    My days in the valley would end.

The waves that, so ruffled awhile,
    Were, glittering, dash'd in the sun,
Oh the bordering violets smile,
    And kiss them, and murmuring run.

Thus let me the splendor and strife
    Of the rich and exalted forego;
With beauty still sweeten my life,
    And love's gentle storm only know!

What joy the Bee-murmurs impart!
    The zephyrs that curl the blue waves!
Soft whispers that steal to the heart!
    And echo that talks in the caves!

Peace, Babblers, or only repeat
    The silver descant of the springs;
Fond shepherds frame here no deceit,
    But scandal has numerous wings.

I call'd you to witness, tis true,
    The vows to Amelia I swore,
Methinks still her blushes I view,
    And, trembling, forgiveness implore.

Her charms I will grave on my heart,
    Her name upon every tree;
And sooner shall love want a dart,
    Than fickleness harbour with me.

'You may Judge from this slight specimen what an excellently fine poet my Don Pedro was; but, alas! I shall never behold him more, O Heavens! Here the amiable Amelia fell into a strong hysteric fit, from which it was with the utmost difficulty that the celestial Arabella, with the assistance of Margaret Grimes, could recover her.'

X

The Fair Siranger's Story Continued

When the divine Amelia had in some degree recovered her spirits, with an eye of expressive languor cast upon Arabella, she thus continued her most interesting narrative. 'My mind, dear madam, as you may well suppose, was perplexed by a thousand alarming apprehensions; I trembled lest the tale should transpire, yet my wounded pride would scarcely suffer me to conceal it.[11] The idea of being in the power of a man, though in fact my husband; the indelicacy, if not disgrace, that would attach itself to my name, for having ventured so far, and so imprudently towards the precipice of destruction, the contempt I must inevitably excite in the mind of Don Pedro, and the idea of practising so unworthy a deception towards my adored mamma, so preyed upon my spirits, that my delicate frame yielded to anxiety, which in a few hours, brought on an alarming and delirious fever.

'There happened fortunately to be a physician on board, who at my mother's instigation, kindly offered his salutary aid, though his humane attention has proved in the end, most fatal to my repose. From the first moment he beheld me, the captivating graces of my person and demeanour fascinated the heart of Don Gomez d'Aldova, for that was his name.[12] The natural fierceness of his character softened before the irresistible attractions of virtue and benignity. An unusual sensation of exquisite delight penetrated his mind, and the engaging anxiety I evinced for the success of his prescriptions, served only to augment the admiration I had inspired.

'Love has that sweet, that undescribable power, which gives mildness to ferocity, and resolution to instability; it humbles the proudest, and exalts the meekest; the libertine is awed by its influence, and the man of feeling adds dignity to his being, by following its dictates. The tenderness of refined sympathy, the rapture of conferring happiness, the conscious delight

---

[11] The source for this passage to the end of the paragraph was Robinson, I: 72-3. Griebel, 382.

[12] This passage to the end of the paragraph and the quotation in the following paragraph derive from Robinson, I: 77-8. Griebel, 382.

of expunging from the soul every vicious propensity, by the dispassionate councils of reason and penetration, are the peculiar attributes of a beloved object. The most dulcet tones, the most sublime efforts of persuasive eloquence, and the tinsel blandishments of empty sophistry, vanish before the resistless influence of the voice we love! It has the power to harmonise the feelings with undescribable magic, leading the senses captive, till every idea is fascinated with the spells of admiration and esteem.' As the matchless Amelia uttered the foregoing enthusiastic rhapsody with almost superhuman energy, so it suddenly overpowered her weak nerves, and she again fell senseless to the floor, while the sympathising Arabella wiped a lambent tear from her finely suffused eye, with a clean cambric handkerchief, and then again administered her benign relief to the fair evanescent stranger.

XI

The Fair Stranger Continues Her Story

Being come to herself, the captivating Amelia thus proceeded in her clear and extraordinary narrative, having first begged pardon, of the languishing Arabella for the alarm and trouble she had occasioned: 'After a tedious voyage, in which our vessel encountered many dreadful storms, we arrived in safety at Falmouth, when my ever honored mamma and myself were received by Mr. Oldfield, a cousin of my father's, with all the kindness and hospitality which so eminently characterize the English nation.

'There was in the house a Miss Ford who was rather approaching to that period when old maidishness begins; she, observing my dejection in consequence of Don Pedro's neglect, which now alas! became too well ascertained, thought proper to introduce to my acquaintance a Captain Beville, a nephew of hers, and who was a young man of most elegant manners. Indeed, my dear, he was uncommonly handsome, sensible, and engaging. Yet the first introduction was in some degree owing to an accident, for he was thrown from his horse at our door, and having fainted away, was in consequence brought into the parlour, and laid upon a blue damask sopha, when I unfortunately entered. The crimson fountain of life had scarcely spread its soft tints upon his pallid lips, when his languid eyes were fixed in speechless extasy on the countenance of your poor Amelia, whose cheek met his gaze as the meek rose encounters the burning glances of the meridian sun![13] Overpowered by his admiration, I was preparing to depart, when the Captain fearful of losing the sight of so charming an object, in a feeble voice accompanied by the most impressive manner entreated me to stay, 'beauteous lady' said he 'if thou art indeed a mortal, for thy outward form bears the strong resemblance of divinity, suffer me for a moment to enjoy the Elysium that presents itself before me: surely I am in the castle of inchantment, and thou art the fair mistress of the air-built habitation! if my returning faculties do not deceive me, I awake from the shades of death to taste the supreme felicities of a terrestrial paradise!'

---

[13] This passage to the end of the paragraph was borrowed from Robinson, I: 27-8. Griebel, 381.

'Miss Ford who witnessed this eloquent harangue, cast a look of soft sympathy upon my heaving bosom, and seemed anxiously to expect my reply, but supper was just bringing in, and the two Miss Maddox's joined our party, who with their usual good nature wished to give a more lively turn to the conversation. I, however, was too much affected by the scene before me, and hastily retired to my mamma's chamber, where I found her in a very languishing condition, the gout which had first seized all her limbs, having now settled in her head, and occasioned the most excruciating tortures. But O! they did not long afflict her, for on the third day, she grew much worse, and towards evening expired, leaving me alone and unprotected in a cruel world, to struggle with my fate.'

Here Amelia's tears began to flow afresh, and the gentle Arabella answered them by her sighs, while Margaret Grimes with louder and more piercing notes, joined the melancholy concert of Affliction.

XII

The Fair Stranger's Story Concluded

After a short pause the mild Amelia thus continued her narrative. 'I confess with some degree of shame, my dear lady, that Captain Beville occupied my thoughts more than perhaps I ought to acknowledge, all circumstances considered, but Don Pedro's conduct had in a great degree alienated my affection, for the blossoms of true love spread their full sails before the gales of prosperity, but cannot resist the tempestuous ocean of adversity. It happened that on a fine summer's evening I went to pay a visit without my mamma to a Mr. Gifford, a gentleman somewhat known in the literary world, and who has written a satirical poem called the Baviad.[14] This terrible writer who modestly stiles himself the modern Perseus, is a little sour looking fellow but prodigiously powerful with his pen, for he is desperately severe, and though he cannot write a line of genuine poetry himself, yet he is extremely alert in abusing those who can. He was formerly a metaphorical bear-leader to my Lord Belgrave, and after his return from the Continent, became literally the tutor of a real bear which his lordship had brought home with him, and which was one of the valuable acquisitions he had made on his travels. Now you must know that one day Mr. Gifford, being negligent of his charge, suffered the bear to eat a whole basket of butter, which the butter-man had left in the passage: this threw his lordship into a great passion, and he immediately discharged the tutor for his carelessness, and placed the hopeful pupil under a more attentive master. It was at this period I paid my visit, and the poor man was quite in a fury at his disgrace, in having his bear taken from him, and consequently he devoted himself to satire, by way of revenge. In this man's society I passed several pleasant hours, and almost forgot the dangers that surrounded me, when unfortunately Captain Beville

---

[14] William Gifford (1756-1826), established a reputation as a vitriolic satirist with the publication of *Baviad* (1791) and *Mæviad* (1795), the first volume, written in the style of Perseus, aimed at attacking the emotional excesses of the Della Cruscan poets of which Robert Merry (1755-1798), Hannah Cowley (1743-1809) and Hester Piozzi (1741-1821) were leaders; the second volume targeted contemporary dramatists. Beckford also refers to the fact that Gifford served as a 'bear-leader,' or travelling tutor, to Robert Grosvenor (1767-1845), Viscount Belgrave. The story of the bear that Beckford recounts is in all likelihood a fiction designed simply to ridicule both Gifford and Belgrave.

arrived: at sight of him, my agonies were renewed, and we agreed to meet the week after, at the house of a Mrs. Martin, in Hertfordshire. This you will allow was imprudent, but who can be wise at all times? Let me now hasten to the conclusion of my melancholy tale, and endeavour to describe in proper colours the awful catastrophe that awaited the destiny of the too wretched Amelia. On this very day I was induced to call at Mrs. Martin's aforesaid, at Daisy Place, when wandering through her improvements, which by the bye, discover her to possess the most refined taste; whom should I meet in the hermitage but Captain Beville. O my friend! think on my situation. He caught me in his arms and vowing eternal love imprinted a thousand amorous kisses on my lips. Just heavens! the crisis of my fate was at hand.—The dog barked, I looked up, and saw the enraged Don Pedro with a countenance flashing with fire and indignation, and with a drawn sword in his hand. In a moment Captain Beville lay weltering in his blood, I fled, as you may naturally suppose, till I reached the spot where I had the supreme felicity to meet the mellifluous Arabella; I had been just exclaiming before you appeared, from the divine Milton

> O where else
> Shall I *deform* my *unattainted* feet,
> In the blind *masses* of this *dangled* wood?
> For I an wearied out
> With the long way *resolving* here to lodge
> Under the spreading *flavour* of these pines."[15]

The virtuous and much injured Amelia having brought her forlorn history to a conclusion, began again to weep, and the susceptible Arabella hastened to pour a healing balm into her recent wounds, then kindly led her to her chamber, and wishing her a good night, retired herself also to enjoy the refreshing slumbers of innocence. At the same time Magaret Grimes ascended to her little garret, and the cat slept in the kitchen.

---

[15] A misquotation of lines from Milton's *Comus: A Masque* (1634), ll. 179-84. The misquotation is designed to expose the shallow affectations of Amelia and other people like her. Beckford brings the mistakes to the reader's attention through the use of italics. The actual lines read:

> O where else
> Shall I inform my unacquainted feet
> In the blind mazes of this tangl'd Wood?
> My Brothers when they saw me wearied out
> With this long way, resolving here to lodge
> Under the spreading favour of these Pines. . .

XIII

The Parting

The morning at length arrived, and the friends who had found all the consolation their circumstances admitted of in being together, were now to part; uncertain when or if ever they were to meet again.[16] Amelia sinking as she was under oppression of many present sorrows and future apprehensions, yet found them all deepened by the loss of Arabella, who had so generously assisted her in supporting them, and Arabella felt, that when to soothe the spirits and strengthen the resolution of her friend was no longer her immediate task, she should dwell with more painful and more steady solicitude on her own singular and unfortunate situation.

Margaret Grimes, warmly attached as she was to both, from gratitude and from affection, had no power to speak comfort to either. Early in the morning she had met the chimney sweeper, and had gone through Lucinda Howard's letter: but though her mind sometimes strongly resisted the idea of hasty marriages, she had nothing to offer against it, and could only sigh over the incurable unhappiness with which she saw the future days of friends she so much loved would be clouded.

Silently they all assembled round the breakfast table; but nobody could eat. Alderman Barlow tried to talk of his Maria, of his house, of his farm, of his fortunate prospects, and of his sister's two little girls, whom he had taken home; but there was not one topic on which he could speak, that did not remind him of the obligations he owed to General Barton, and the Howard family, nor one idea which arose unimbittered with the reflection, that they, to whom he was indebted for all *his* happiness, were themselves miserable.

About twelve o'clock Mr. Peter Perkins came into the room in his usual way; and enquired eagerly of Arabella whether she intended going to the races, and whether he could see her there; and without waiting for an answer to his enquiry, told her that he had that morning met Colonel Symes, a

---

[16] This entire chapter was borrowed from Charlotte Smith, *Celestina* (1791). Source identified by Griebel, 384-6. For actual passages, see Loraine Fletcher, ed., *Celestina* (Toronto: Broadview, 2004), 346-8. All references hereafter are to this edition.

particular friend of Henry Lambert, and that Lady Susan Harris had been in the country about a week. Every body who was acquainted with her dear Henry could not fail to be interesting to Arabella, and from Lady Susan she had always supposed more might be collected than from any other person: but now her mind was too much oppressed and too much confused to allow her to distinguish her sensations, or to arrange any settled plan for her future conduct towards Lady Susan. She received Mr. Peter Perkins's information, therefore, with coldness, and indeed her manners towards him were very constrained and distant, which he either did not or would not notice; rattling on in his usual wild way, though he saw the dejection and concern of the party; a circumstance that more than ever disgusted Arabella, who began some time before to doubt whether the credit which Mr. Peter Perkins had for good nature, was not given him on very slender foundations: for to be so entirely occupied by his own pleasures and pursuits, as to be incapable of the least sympathy towards others, to be unable or unwilling to check for one moment his vivacity in compliment to their despondence, seemed to Arabella such a want of sensibility, as gave her a very indifferent opinion of his heart.

Amelia quitted the room to make the last preparations for her departure: but Margaret Grimes who had settled every thing before, remained with Arabella and Mr. Peter Perkins. He would have given the world to have passed these moments in conversation with her, but the presence of a third person, and especially of Margaret Grimes, put an end to all hope he had of an opportunity of explaining to her with that tenderness and caution, which the subject required, some circumstances relative to Henry Lambert's fortune, which had lately come to his knowledge. New embarrassments seemed threatening him, and a law suit, involving part of the property which belonged to the Devonshire estate, appeared likely to increase these embarrassments.

All this Mr. Peter Perkins thought Arabella ought to know, yet in their first interview that morning, he had not courage to tell her of it, and now General Barton had left him no chance of doing it, for while he yet deliberated, the coach sent by the Marchioness of Oakley stopped at the door, and the moment was come in which he was to take his leave of her.

He took her hand, and kissed it with an air of grateful respect; but he could only say, 'I shall write to you in a few days, and I hope, give you a good account of my grandmother, and of little Peggy.'

'I hope you will,' returned Arabella, faintly.

'And,' added he, 'you will of course like to hear of all that passes material in our neighbourhood?'

'Certainly I shall,' replied she. 'Adieu, dear sir. I cannot say much, but you know what I feel for you all.'

The Rev. Mr. Devaynes had taken her hand to lend her down stairs; but she disengaged it from him, and said to Mr. Peter Perkins, as she gave it to *him*, 'Let us go to your sister.' He led her to the door of the room; where at that moment Amelia entered pale and breathless; her eyes were heavy, and fixed on Arabella, but she did not weep. Arabella's tears, however, were more ready, and as she embraced her friend, they choaked the trembling adieu she would have uttered, and fell in showers on her bosom. The emotion was too painful; and Mr. Peter Perkins desirous to end it for both their sakes, disengaged Amelia from the arms of the trembling Arabella, while Mr. Devaynes seizing Amelia by the hand, hurried her down stairs, and as he put her into the coach, told her he should wait upon her the next day. She would have besought him not to do it, as a liberty he ought not to take in the house whither she was going; but before she could sufficiently recover herself to find words, the coach was driven away, and in a short time, she found herself at the door of the Marchioness of Oakley, at Fairy Lodge, and it became necessary for her to collect her spirits, to acquit herself as so much kind attention deserved.

XIV

A Scene of Horror, a Ghost, and a Supper

It is now necessary to return to Henry Lambert, who pursued his journey with unabating perseverance, and at midnight found himself in an immense forest through which there was no tract, and the thickness of which prevented the smallest glimmering of light from penetrating the 'palpable obscure.'[17] On every side were heard strange murmurs as of persons in anguish, and now and then the mournful gale brought to his astonished ear some faint female lamentations. The river had overflowed its banks with a spreading inundation, and the stupendous rocks that seemed to prop the skies, collected dreadful thunders over his head. There appeared to his wondering faculties, to be a chasm in all nature, and the howling wolf, as if conscious of the general desolation of the scene, added terror to the perturbation he endured.

Philip Duvergois his faithful valet was advanced only a few paces, when a bloody spectre with a countenance of the most inconceivable dismay and agony, glided by, bearing in its hand a scroll on which was written—DEATH.—A sudden flash of lightning threw a lustre upon the parchment at the moment. Henry's heart felt involuntary depression, but collecting all his fortitude, he called to Duvergois, saying,—'Saw you that figure, what was it?'—'You ask me vat it vas, by Saint Jeronimo it vas a live ghost.' A long silence now ensued, when the two travellers arrived at an old abbey that was mouldering in decay, and which seemed the abode of some banditti who frequented the forest, as none but the outcasts of society could inhabit so melancholy and dreary an abode.

On approaching the south aisle which was over-run with ivy, and covered with moss, the ornaments of time, Henry's horse began to neigh, and immediately a light appeared at the chapel window and the bell tolled. Henry rushed forward with an animated courage, and in a few seconds, found himself in an ancient hall in which was a table with some covered dishes placed thereon, but no person appeared. A pendant lamp from the fretted roof, discovered to the terrified Henry the awful solemnity of the place. He called Duvergois, but

---

[17] John Milton, *Paradise Lost*, Bk. II, l. 406.

received no answer, when on a sudden an unnatural burst of laughter was heard in the adjoining apartment. Henry, not dismayed, smote with the handle of his sword against the door of the room from whence the noise had issued. Another burst of laughter more shocking than the former struck upon his heart. Anon the portal opened and an appearance so exquisitely horrible presented itself to his sight, that all resolution failed him, and he fled. Henry traversed the great hall with the swiftness of an Antelope, he arrived at a marble stair-case which he ascended, till he came into a long gallery. By a glimpse of the moon which now darted a transient lustre through an antiquated casement he thought he discovered a female at some distance on her knees before a crucifix. Hs paused, uncertain whether to advance or not, when a man before unseen caught him in his arms. It was Duvergois; 'O mine Got' said he 'let us escape from dis abominable abbey, I have seen de Tifel himself, O my dear master, in dat cell is de body of a murdered man, I saw him lie dere gashed vit vounds, O vat will become of us?' During this parley, a child of about seven years of age came out of a small closet on the right side of the gallery with a lighted torch in his hand. The infant looked earnestly in Henry's face and said 'will you come to the banquet, supper is served up, there are only seven; the widow, my dear mother, is at prayers, but the Baron will be there, and I wish the soup may please your palates.' They now followed the child in speechless amazement till they arrived at a spacious saloon, round which were arrayed a number of figures in armour; the infant pointed to them and exclaimed 'Henry Lambert, these may all be called your predecessors, for they came hither and departed no more.' At these words he gave a loud shriek and disappeared, leaving Henry and Duvergois to ruminate on what had passed. It was totally dark, yet the near and frequent trampling of feet convinced them that there were persons moving about. 'Who passes there?' said Henry. 'Only your lordship's servants,' replied a female voice, 'who are going to bid the strangers welcome, and to give them the reception you wish, be not uneasy, my lord! they will soon be safe.' Immediately after, a large pair of folding doors at the end of the saloon flew open, and discovered seven persons at supper, five ladies and two gentlemen, all magnificently dressed, but masked: there were two vacant seats, which surprized Henry, as it appeared that he and Duvergois were expected to complete the party. One of the ladies on observing the two travellers, left the table and lightly tripping towards them, took Henry gracefully by the hand, and presented him to the company, saying 'This courteous gentleman deserves your notice, his attendant also shall partake of our repast. Worthy strangers be seated, you may depend upon having excellent fare with us, those who visit us never know how to leave us.' The masked figure who sat at the head of the table now helped Henry and Duvergois to some soup, and earnestly entreated them to fall to, which they did somewhat reluctantly notwithstanding the keenness of their appetites. One of the ladies after a little while took a rose from her bosom and presented it to Henry at the same time singing with great sweetness the following lines:

> With blushing modesty she glows,
> And from her bosom takes a rose,
> Accept my Corydon! she cries,
> With sweetest look, and downcast eyes;
> Accept from me this fading flower—
> *He* scarce can live another hour,
> Yet while 'tis fresh, O let it be
> A dear remembrancer of me!
>> Rash sleep,
>> Slash deep,
>> Loory loory loo.

A loud and general applause testified the company's delight at this song, and in a little time afterwards, the principal male figure chaunted with a bass voice the ensuing stanza.

> The Muses nine, and Graces three,
> Do all unanimous agree:
> The Muses first, that all they can impart
> Of excellence is in your heart;
> That all their wit and sense is in your mind
> Pure as the golden ore, and as refined:
> The Graces next, with reverence declare,
> By merit you have ta'en their shape and air,
> Thus the Nine Muses in your mind we see,
> And in your lovely form the Graces Three.
>> Ever dare,
>> Never spare,
>> Hooly, cooly, kill.

This last song occasioned a vast expansion of merriment, when one of the ladies dropped her mask.—Henry in astonishment cried out 'What! Miss Louisa Singleton?' To which she replied, 'Yes, sir, the very same whom you used to visit at her papa's, near Rochester.' All the company now unmasked, and the Duke de Belcour explained the whole joke, Madame Lebon rallying

Henry prodigiously on his late alarm. They all enquired eagerly after Arabella, and the nature of his hopes. He gave than in consequence a full account of the last campaign, and then taking Madamoiselle Roubilliere by the hand, began the ball without further ceremony. The peasants of the neighbouring districts hastened at the sound of the merry tabor, and Duvergois watched an opportunity to give his master's letter to the gardiner, with the strictest injunction to be careful. The pictures now were all brought out and examined with a critical eye both by the corporal and the innkeeper, on which account the sale was deferred till the morrow, and the Commandant politely invited them all to dinner on the succeeding Tuesday.

So ended this tragical adventure, and Henry's spirits having been recruited by nine hours sleep, he attended the parade with more than his usual alacrity, thus dedicating his soul to honor and Arabella, and proving at least the truth of the sublime lines in Cato.

'Tis not for mortals to command success,
But we'll do more, Sempronius, we'll deserve it.[18]

---

[18] Joseph Addison, *Cato: A Tragedy*, I, ii, ll. 44-5.

XV

The Struggles of Virtue Prevail

For several days Arabella devoted her whole thoughts to her dearly beloved Henry, and regretted more and more the fatal cause of their separation. Sometimes grief would rise to its achmé in her mind, and she was frantic with despair; again she would sink into the soft calm of melancholy. But time with its rapid wing kept flying by, yet brought her no intelligence of the object that most interested her feeling heart. At the end of the week, however, she received a letter from the valuable suffering Amelia; but O! what was the agitation of her mind when she perused the contents.

The Letter

'My dear, amiable, lovely and excellent Arabella,

For the future I will always mistrust most when appearances look fairest. O your poor friend! what has she not suffered since she left you, and Oh! you shall hear what a vile and unwomanly part that wicked Marchioness has acted. Take, then, the dreadful story, as well as I can relate it.[19]

The maid Martha is a little apt to drink if she can get at liquor, and having chanced to find a bottle of cherry brandy, the wench drank more of it than she should, for which she was soundly rated by the Marchioness, who ordered her to go and sleep off her liquor before we came to bed.

About two hours after, which was near eleven o'clock, the Marchioness and I went up to go to bed; I pleasing myself with what a charming night I should have. Poor Martha was sitting fast asleep, in an elbow chair, in a dark corner of the room, with her apron thrown over her head and neck. The Marchioness said, 'there is that beast of a wench fast asleep, instead of being abed!' I knew, she

---

[19] Almost the entire letter that follows came from Samuel Richardson's well-known account of the attempted rape of Pamela with Beckford's own modifications to create a comic effect in his version. For passages, see William M. Sale, ed., *Pamela or Virtue Rewarded* (New York: W. W. Norton, 1958), 208-14. Source first identified by Frank Gees Black, *The Epistolary Novel in the Late Eighteenth Century* (Eugene: University of Oregon, 1940), 99.

had taken a fine dose.' 'I'll wake her,' said I. 'No don't,' said she, 'let her sleep on, we shall lie better without her,' and indeed I thought so, for it appeared to me rather strange to sleep three in a bed.

The Marchioness by this time was got to-bed, on the farther side, to make room for the maid when she should awake. I got into bed and lay close to her. 'Put your arm under mine,' said the wicked Marchioness; so I did, and the abominable Lady held my hand with her right-hand, as my right arm was under her left.

In less than a quarter of an hour, I said, 'There's poor Martha awake, I hear her stir.' 'Let us go to sleep,' said her Ladyship, 'and not mind her.'

At that, Martha sat down by the bed-side and began to undress. I heard her, as I thought, breathe all quick and short: 'Indeed,' said I, 'the poor maid is not well; what ails you, Mrs. Martha?' but no answer was given.

But I shudder to relate it. She came into bed, trembling like an Aspen-leaf, and I, poor fool that I was, pitied her much. What words shall I find, my dear Arabella, to describe the rest, and my confusion, when the guilty wretch, (who was no other than Lord Mahogany himself) took my left arm, and laid it under his neck, and the vile Marchioness held my right, and then he clasped me round the waist.

Said I 'Is the wench mad? Why how now Confidence!' thinking still it had been Martha. But he kissed me with frightful vehemence; and then his voice broke upon me like a clap of thunder. 'Now Amelia,' said his Lordship, 'is the dreadful time of reckoning come.' I screamed out in such a manner, as never any body heard the like. But there was nobody to help me, and both my hands were secured, as I said. Sure never poor soul was in such agonies as I.

Says he, 'One word with you, Amelia! hear me but one word, and hitherto you see I offer nothing to you?' 'Is this *nothing*?' said I, 'to be in bed here? to hold my hands between you! I *will hear*, if you will both instantly leave the bed.'

Said the Marchioness (O disgrace of womankind!) 'What you do, my Lord, do; don't stand dilly-dallying; she cannot exclaim worse than she has done: and she'll be quieter when she knows the worst.'

He now put his hand in my bosom: with struggling and sorrow I fainted away quite, and did not come to myself soon; so that they both, from the cold sweats that I was in, thought me dying.

Your poor Amelia cannot answer for the liberties taken with her, in her deplorable state of death, but when I recovered my senses, his Lordship solemnly, and with a bitter imprecation vowed that he had not offered the least indecency, that he was frightened at the terrible manner I was taken with the fit: that he should desist from his attempt; and begged but to see me easy and quiet, and he would leave me directly and go to his own bed. 'O then,' said I, 'take with you this vile Marchioness, as an earnest that I may believe you.'

'And will you, my Lord,' said the wicked Lady, 'for a fit or two, give up such an opportunity as this? I thought you had known the sex better. She is now, you see, quite well again!'

This I heard; more she might say; but I fainted away once more, at these words, and at his clasping his arms about me again. When I came a little to myself, I found that his Lordship was gone, and Mrs. Dorothy Webster holding a smelling bottle to my nose, and no Marchioness.

This O my beloved Arabella, was a most dreadful trial! I tremble still to think of it, and dare not recal all the horrid circumstances, though I hope, as his lordship assures me, that he was not guilty of indecency.

I shall leave this naughty house tomorrow, and go to my cousin Filby's at Margate. I fear you will not think the lace fine enough, but it was the test the picklesalmon man had to dispose of, or you may be sure I should have waited till Miss St. George had returned from the north; but that not having been the case, I will no longer trespass on your patience than to subscribe myself, dearest Arabella,

Your truly affectionate

AMELIA DE GONZALES.'
Fairy-Lodge, Friday 17th.

Having perused this lamentable epistle, the blooming Arabella wrapped in the insensibility of private sorrow, suffered herself to be arrayed for dinner. Serene dejection sat upon her countenance, and her mild eyes were expressive of the resignation she had imposed upon a heart alive to every sentiment of friendship and benevolence.

As soon as dinner was at an end, Arabella, in company with the eldest Miss Appleby, took a walk upon the common, and near farmer Rigby's stile, she observed a small piece of folded paper on the ground, which she took up, and to her great surprize, found it to contain the following lively verses addressed to herself.

To the Heavenly Miss Arabella Bloomville

What proof shall I give of my passion,
    Or how shall I struggle with fate?

Arabella! since cards came in fashion,
   You've mark'd me an object of hate.

I'd have willingly fought with the devil,
   And grateful have been, to be slain,
For I suffer indefinite evil,
   And warble alone to complain.

Like a madman I scour o'er the vallies,
   Unobserv'd like a mite in a cheese,
For 'tis the criterion of malice
   To laugh at my efforts to please.

Now I snuff the fresh air of the morning,
   In a transport of sorrow—because
You treat me with flouting and scorning,
   But hold, it is time I should pause.

Endymion

Arabella now returned home more tranquil and serene than she had been for many months.

XVI

A Mistake, and a Most Interesting Arrival

It was one of those soft mild evenings when scarcely a wandering zephyr presumes to disturb the tranquility of nature. The setting sun had thrown a yellow glow on the huge masses of grey marble, whose crevices here and there afforded a scanty subsistence to lichens and moss campion, while the desolate barrenness of other parts added to that threatening aspect with which they seemed to hang over the wandering traveller, when Henry leaping from his horse, cast himself at the foot of an aged oak, in a state between indifference and despair. 'How long' cried he 'am I to be the sport of fortune, how long separated from the arms of the angelic Arabella the sole mistress of my heart? Had my uncle Parkinson foreseen my sufferings, he would never have permitted the base triumph of Lord Mahogany to have embittered all my hopes, nor have relied upon the promises of Sir Matthew Sullivan to extricate me from my difficulties. Peace will now probably be soon established, and those who fell in battle will be mourned in vain, more especially since the ridiculous and disastrous war has been so completely unsuccessful.[20] Yet what of that? If I return home can I be sure of the settled consolation which all my endeavours have tended to procure me? Is not General Barton my bitter enemy, and can I stand alone against so powerful a confederacy?'

Here an involuntary sigh escaped him, for he looked back with soft regret to those times, when Mrs. Marmaduke cherished his youthful propensities in her sweet retirement. He called to mind the interesting period when the tear of friendship bedewed her bridal eye—suddenly he recollected that she was now no more, that she was alas! the silent tenant of the grave. The conflict was too much to bear, for his love for Arabella was more ardent than ever, and the pangs of absence more insupportable.

While therefore determined to unbosom himself to his friend Fergusson, and consult with him what was best to be done in the present crisis of his

---

[20] The war with France that had begun in 1793 and was continuing without resolution, causing unrest throughout England.

situation. Fergusson he knew to be a tall well-looking young man with a good heart and an excellent understanding, but he dreaded lest the influence of some artful female might draw his secret forth, if he should confide in him too far, and thus ruin all his projects. At times indeed he felt some little indignation both against Jennings and him for the trick they had put upon him relative to the venison feast, but that matter had now blown over, and he generously made allowances for their inconsiderate inattention.

While he was yet wavering, the landlord waited upon him, and offered to purchase his greyhounds, assuring him at the same time, that Lord Thomas Groves had slept there the night before, and had praised the wine very much.

Henry however was deaf to all his entreaties, and totally forgot to make the necessary enquiries after Lucinda Howard, which mortified the old Baronet's pride a good deal, for though he was of an open jovial character, yet he knew the value of land as well as any man, and had absolutely refused a peerage from principle.

In a paroxysm of grief therefore Henry retired early to his chamber, and calling for a boiled fowl and a bottle of Burton ale, in a few hours composed the following beautiful acrostic, as a tribute of admiration and esteem to the unrivalled excellence of Arabella.

Lines Addressed to the Lovely Arabella

May all the gods approve my tender love,
Yes, all the gods, the Pagan gods above!
Wise she is truly, gentle, good, and kind
In body active, and sublime in mind;
Fond as a turtle dove—O may she be
Eternally, what this acrostic means, to me! [21]

The waiter now ran into the room with a note, which he said a little boy had that moment left at the bar—Henry broke open the seal with eager anxiety and read as follows:

'My dear friend,

It is with great grief, I confess, that I heard, the quantity of goose you ate yesterday has occasioned you a pain in your side; you should keep yourself

---

[21] A verse in which the initial or final letters of the lines taken in order form a word or phrase. In this case, it is 'MY WIFE.'

warm by a good fire, and sit quiet in an elbow chair. I have seen a receipt for this disorder in a book that is now out of print. But I will not tire your patience any further; lest you grow melancholy, and lose the memory of former amusements, which we are apt to regret when they have taken flight from us. I shall therefore lay down my pen for the present, though I would resume it in a second, had I any good news to send you.

I am, dear Doctor,
Yours affectionately,
BRIDGET CAWTHORNE.'

Henry Lambert was very much irritated by this foolish mistake, and cursing heartily both the Doctor and Bridget Cawthorne, stepped into a post chaise, and desiring the lad to make all possible haste, fell asleep in the corner, while his still active imagination was delighted with the hovering phantom of Arabella. The blush of innocence, the glow of artless beauty, bloomed on her cherub cheek, the milk of sweetness hung upon her tongue.

In the mean time, Arabella had not been out long before the chill and gloomy appearance encreased, and darkness coming on, she slowly and reluctantly returned to the house.[22] She heard a little before she quitted the road, the rattling of a chaise, but not attending to it, she did not even distinguish whether it might belong to any person of the place, or to some traveller. She entered the parlour, and sat down by the card table, where the Earl having performed his evening's task, had just resigned his place to Mr. McIntosh. Suddenly a voice was heard in the passage, enquiring for Lady Langley. 'My Lady is within sir,' replied the man. 'And who are with her?' 'The Earl of Pocklington, Mr. Paul Dodsworth, Mrs. Kemp, the three Miss Bernards, Doctor Browne, Miss Bloomville, General Barton, Sir Obediah Loftus'—the servant was going on, when the enquirer said vehemently, 'It is enough—let me however see them.' Arabella at the sound of this voice, had started from her chair—the second sentence it uttered, affected her still more; but she had no time to answer the eager enquiry of Mr. Thomas Jackson, 'What is the matter?' before the parlour door opened; and pale, breathless, with an expression to which only the pencil can do justice, she saw before her the figure of Henry Lambert.

There was agony and desperation in his looks. He gasped, like a fish in fits—he would have spoken but could not. The company all rose in silence.

---

[22] This sentence to the end of the chapter was taken from Smith's *Celestina*, 530-1. Griebel, 386-8.

Lady Langley who hardly knew him even by sight, looked at Arabella for an explanation, which she was unable to give.—At length, Henry, as if by an effort of passionate phrenzy, approached Arabella, and said in a hurried and inarticulate way, 'I would speak to you, Madam,—though—to—this gentleman, I suppose,' and he turned to General Barton, 'I must apply for permission.'

Arabella could not conjecture why he looked so little in his senses—She sat down—for her limbs refused to support her—and faintly said or tried to say, 'I hope I see Captain Lambert well.'

Lady Langley then addressed herself to him—desired him to take a chair, and to do her the honor of staying supper with her. He heard or heeded her not—but, with fixed eyes, gazing on Arabella, he struck his hands together, and cried—while the violence of his emotion choked him—'It is all over then—I have lost her—and have nothing to do here—No, by heaven, I cannot bear it.' He then turned away, and left the room as hastily as he had entered it.

'My dear Arabella!' cried lady Langley, 'what does all this mean? Do, General Barton—for Miss Bloomville is, I perceive, much alarmed—do, speak to Mr. Lambert—I am really concerned to see him in such a situation.'

'No,' said Arabella, who would not for the world have had General Barton follow him—'No; I will go myself after him.' Her fears gave her resolution, and without heeding General Barton, who would have prevented her, she hurried after Henry, and overtook him just as he was quitting the house.

'Dear sir,' said she, 'Dear Henry!' At those well known sounds once so precious to him, he turned round—She took his hand—'I am very sorry to see you' continued she, 'in such agitation of spirits—I am afraid something is wrong.'

'Wrong,' cried he, 'wrong! and do you Arabella, inhuman Arabella, insult me with such an enquiry? Wrong!—am I not the most cursed of human beings?'

'I hope not' interrupted she, 'for your happiness'—she knew no longer what she meant to say; nor did he give her time to recollect; for eagerly rivetting his eyes on her face, and grasping her hands between his—he cried 'My happiness!—and what of my happiness? Is it not gone, lost for ever?—Have you not destroyed it? Damnation and distraction—Why do I linger here?' He then plunged away, and rushed out of the door, where Duvergois waited for him with the chaise.

XVII

Regret and Lamentation

General Barton's grandmother had been long in a declining state, and for the last thirty years had afforded little hopes of a permanent recovery—but she was now rapidly approaching

> That undiscovered country, from whose bourne,
> No traveller returns.[23]

Lucinda Howard descended hastily to fetch the General—prepared him for the pity-moving spectacle, and introduced him to his dying grandmother. She had requested to be raised, and supported by her pillows: strong agitation convulsed her frame, and, for a few moments, she was deprived of the power of utterance. An interval of calm succeeded—she extended her emaciated arms.—The General who understood the sign, suffered her to embrace him; the drops of soft humanity, wrung from his feeling heart, fell upon her cheek. A ghostly smile illumined her haggard eyes—she loosed her feeble hold—then faintly articulated 'I am forgiven, I am happy!' and sinking on her pillow, instantly expired.

A scene so mournful, and a death so sudden, awfully affected the gay Sir Charles Atkinson, and the lovely Lucinda Howard. The General supported the latter from the breathless corpse of his grandmother. Lady Langley was no less shocked at an event, little expected to take place so soon. She sent a complimentary message, but was herself too much indisposed to admit an interview. At length, being tolerably recovered, she was attended to the carriage by her two companions, and set out on her return to London. The spirits of this amiable woman had been so much affected by the penitence and death of Lady Barton, for whom she once felt the tenderest friendship, that she was some time confined to her chamber. There she shed fresh tears to the renewed remembrance of her beloved husband, whose injurious conduct never could erase him from her affections.

---

[23] Shakespeare. [Beckford's note]. See *Hamlet*, III, i, ll. 79-80.

During this interval, Mr. Simon Walford, the steward of the late Lady Barton, attended his new master, who was soon fixed in the secure possession of the inheritance of his ancestors: but the General was dead to every pleasure fortune could bestow. This amiable man whose attentions during her illness, and anxiety for her recovery, could not have been exceeded even towards the wife of his choice, was sensibly touched by her sudden fate![24]—With undissembled tears he mourned her death, and tenderly regretted her removal from a world, to which she had been too fondly attached! In contemplating the ghastly form, that once glowed with animated beauty, how does the thinking mind moralize upon the vanity of short-lived pleasures!

The grief, the anguish of the General, is not to be described; that heart alone can sympathize with such sensations, which has experienced such a loss. The revival of his grandmother's virtues obliterated the impression of her failings:—he remembered only the dignity of her form, and the graces of her mind!—nor could all his philosophic resolution support with fortitude, this unexpected stroke of fortune! He felt, bereaved of every social joy, the comfort of his life—deserted and forlorn! Thus the fair blooming branches cropped from the venerable tree, are left unsheltered, to the rude elements and boisterous tempest!

Scarce could the gentle force of friendship drag this heart-stricken General from the deformed remains of what was once his grandmother. Fixed like a statue, he gazed upon her face! then smote his gallant breast, and with a smile of anguish thus exclaimed.

'Yes, it is past! the only tie of nature that remained to attach me to existence, is now dissolved!—Life has no more a charm, nor death a pang for me! O thou who lately wert so kind, so talkative, so venerable!—thou art fled for ever—the ravages of sickness have defaced thine awe-inspiring wrinkles, and left thee a spectacle of horror! O my grandmother! my grandmother!'

Thus did the afflicted General vent his soul's anguish; neither when borne from this scene of desolation, did his piercing lamentation cease:—still he addressed the invisible object of his sorrows, till overwhelmed with grief, he sunk into a silent stupor.

Several gentlemen of a neighbouring county who were only acquainted with her Ladyship's merit, but had no personal knowledge of her, caused an elegant marble monument to be erected to her memory in Langley church, and one of the first poets of the age furnished the following beautiful epitaph, which

---

[24] This sentence to the end of the paragraph and the following four paragraphs were borrowed from the sentimental novel, *Julia de Gramont* (London, 1788), II: 289-93, by Baroness Cassandra Hawke (1746-1813) of Towton. Identified by Griebel, 393-4.

for dirge-like simplicity, and striking pathos, has seldom been equalled, and never excelled. Every line goes directly to the heart. Lady Barton had a fine poetical vein herself, and had unfortunately been subject to fits of insanity, besides which it is reported of her, that in her latter days she would never read any book but the bible. All these circumstances are feelingly touched upon by the above-mentioned bard.

The Epitaph[25]

> Ye who the merits of the dead revere,
> Who hold misfortune sacred, genius dear,
> Regard this tomb, where Lady Barton's name
> Solicits kindness with a double claim!
> Tho' nature gave her, and tho' science taught
> The fire of fancy, and the reach of thought;
> Severely, doom'd to suffer grief's extreme,
> She pass'd, in madd'ning pain, life's fev'rish dream;
> While rays of genius only serv'd to shew
> The thick'ning horror, and exalt her woe.
> Ye walls that eccho'd to her frantic moan,
> Guard the due records of this grateful stone!
> Strangers to her, enamour'd of her lays,
> This fond memorial to her talents raise.
> For this the ashes of a Fair require
> Who touch'd the tend'rest notes of pity's lyre;
> Who join'd pure faith to strong poetic powers,
> Who in reviving reason's lucid hours
> Sought on one book her troubled mind to rest,
> And rightly deem'd the book of God the best.

---

[25] This epitaph was written by William Hayley (1745-1820) and John Sargeant (d. 1831) to the memory of William Collins (1721-1759) for a monument erected in Chichester to the poet, a native of that city. The monument was executed by John Flaxman (1755-1826) in 1795 and placed in the city's cathedral. Beckford inserts Lady Barton's name for Collins and describes her final days to coincide with the prevailing view that Collins suffered from mental illness and turned to the Bible for solace just before he died. An engraving of Flaxman's monument was published in August 1796 and appeared as the frontispiece to the *European Magazine*, XXX (1796). The epitaph inscribed on the monument appeared in *The Gentleman's Magazine*, LXV, pt. 2 (September, 1795): 742.

XVIII

New Characters, and
a Learned Dissertation

Mrs. De Malthe[26] was a Lady of very shining qualities, and the finest aristocratic sensations; her noble ambition was to form splendid connections, and to be admitted into the society of the great. To gratify this wise wish, she sacrificed all other considerations. She wrote books, she gave balls and concerts, and she dressed, for no other purpose, but the attainment of this her favourite object. She was fully and properly persuaded that kings can do no wrong, and that they were authorized by heaven to massacre and plunder their own subjects, and to desolate the world at their pleasure. She professed herself the most loyal of all human Beings; was a praiseworthy, orthodox believer, yet with religious enthusiasm she would have doomed all men to the flames, who even suffered themselves to doubt on any article of faith which she had adopted. For the majority of mankind, who languish in hovels, and wither away by hard labour, she had little compassion. She thought that they were only sent into the world to pay tithes and taxes, and by their incessant exertions to procure luxuries and amusements for the rich and powerful. To be distinguished as a woman of learning, she had ransacked all the indexes of books of science, and of the classics; her writings and discourse were larded with scraps of Latin and Greek, with far-fetched allusions, and obsolete quotations. Her manners were affectedly easy, and vulgarly refined; she was also more remarkable for her professions of sincerity, than for the sincerity of her professions. In her conversation she was frequently lively and sometimes entertaining, and at all times knew better how to please than to attach. She

---

[26] André Parreaux believed that Mrs De Malthe was a caricature of Hester Thrale Piozzi (1741-1821). See 'The Caliph and the Swinish Multitude,' in *William Beckford of Fonthill, Bicentenary Essays*, ed. Fatma Mahmoud, *Supplement to Cairo Studies in English*, 1960, 5. While Parreaux did not explain why he made this identification, there seems to be support for it in the text. De Malthe appears to be a veiled reference to Piozzi's first husband's 'malt' factory or brewery in Southwark. Piozzi was also a staunch political and religious conservative 'fully and properly persuaded that kings can do so wrong,' She had a penchant for pretentiously displaying her erudition in public and in her written works, which she would often 'lard' with 'scraps' of Latin and Greek, and she also retired to Wales in 1795 as did Mrs De Malthe. In addition, Beckford pokes fun at her writing style at the end of this chapter.

had confirmed all her old prejudices by travelling, and had acquired new ones, and hated a philosopher as much as she feared the devil.

To this Lady, who was now retired into Wales, having been disgusted by the neglect of the fashionable world, the interesting and lovely Miss Lucinda Howard went to pay a visit, hoping, amidst the wild scenery of mountains and natural cascades, to be able to indulge her romantic passion more tranquilly, than she could do among large assemblies, and the public amusements of high life.

Mrs. De Malthe received her with smiles and apparent gratitude, and endeavoured to soothe her tender grief, by every species of rural entertainment. She introduced her to all her Welch friends, and strove to gratify her by Cambrian festivity, but in vain—the penetrating flame of jealousy had congealed her heart, and the lightning flashes of struggling virtue dragged her heavily on through a chaos of disappointment. The lake might bubble on the valley's breast, or the pine-grove shake its hoary honours through the glade, but without effect. The distant water-fall lost its mild murmurs in the air, and feebly died upon her senses.

Lucinda felt with additional anxiety for the fate of her Arabella, and mingling her friend's sensations with her own, arrived speedily at that state of rending apathy, when the nerves relax before the tempest of disappointment.

Musick and poetry were now her only resources, but from these she found occasional relief, from these she learnt that solemn patience which submits to what it cannot resist, and flies from an ungrateful and turbulent world, to the calm and silent abyss of solitude and oblivion.

Henry's duel, she well knew, must rend the feelings of the too susceptible Arabella, with ineffable distress, and though the consequences had been less fatal than might at first have been suspected, yet she dared not mention the circumstance to Mrs. De Malthe, lest her extatic sensibility should be shaken in the extreme.

She sometimes thought of hastily returning to the metropolis, but then again her heart failed her, and she determined to carry the secret with her to the grave.

On one of these awful occasions, she composed the subsequent poem, which Mrs. De Malthe declared, was equal in imagery to any of the most admired works of Jeremiah Drexelius[27] himself, had all the rich colouring which distinguished the animated pencil of Giotto,[28] and was indeed a bright exanthema[29] of the muse.

---

[27] Jeremias Drexel (1581-1638), Jesuit priest and author of works of devotional literature. He was fond of pictorial symbols to illustrate his teachings. His first book *De aeternitate considerations* (1620) was devoted to various representations of eternity.

[28] Giotto di Bondone (c. 1267-1337), Florentine painter and founder of the Italian school of painting.

[29] Quite literally an eruption, or rash—a disease characterized by efflorescence.

The Poem

Where will at last my wretched wand'rings end?
Where shall I find contentment and a friend?
Not such as grandeur, in its polish'd trim,
Tends honest faith in charities of whim:
Not such as Clodio,[30] with a boasting mood,
Affords his nearest relatives in blood;
Whom famish'd nature to his gates has borne,
The bitter pittance of his hand to mourn:
Not such as sycophants from fools obtain,
The transient earnest of a venal strain!
Or new created insolence affords[31]
Mongrels in rank, and visionary lords!
But such as freedom, with unclouded mind
Can dare receive, and publish to mankind:
Where friendship, careful of its friend in need,
Prevents the burning blush, and hides the deed.

On every side by disappointment foil'd,
With hopes deceiv'd, and promises turmoil'd,
Misfortune gathers on my sickn'ing eye,
And melancholy prompts the gnawing sigh.
And can my friend, whom heav'n has kindly blest
With ev'ry comfort of the human breast,
Whose dearest pleasure is to soothe distress,
Its sorrow soften, and its sigh repress,
To ease, by stealth the miseries of life,
And scatter roses o'er the thorns of strife—
And can my friend the memory renew
Of scenes to which I breath'd a long adieu!
When anguish visiting secluded care,
Within the deep recesses of despair
Her dwelling takes; ah! what avails it then

---

[30] Clodio (c. 395-447 or 449), a legendary king of the Salian Franks from the Merovingian dynasty. He was an aggressive conqueror of territory that ultimately became the country of France.

[31] Mrs De Malthe rather objected to this and the five following lines as being low, and denoting an improper democratic spirit. [Beckford's note].

To talk of friendship or the ties of men?
Ah! what avails it from ourselves to fly,
Or mingle comfort with affliction's sigh?
Lull'd for a time the bitt'rest grief may rest,
To wake with tenfold anguish in the breast.

And if the solace of De Malthe is vain,
What other balm can mitigate my pain?
Oh that oblivion could enwrap the whole,
And close each information of my soul!
Contented then, this restless heart at ease,
No friends to promise, and no views to tease;
Unknown to all the flatt'ry which beguiles
Full many a youth, and ruins with its smiles;
Unknown to luxury's deceitful ways,
The wanton libertine, the villain's praise,
In rural peace my spotless hours might run,
My wishes equal, and my prospects one!
E'en thou, mad love! thou tyrant of mankind,
Faithless to all, to *me* the most unkind;
Save education, first and direst foe!
From which, with knowledge, all my sorrows flow—
E'en thou mad love! my troubled heart wouldst spare,
And scatter comfort LIKE A RUSSIAN BEAR.

When the tender-hearted Lucinda had finished the reading of her delightful composition, Mrs. De Malthe thus affectionately addressed her.[32]

'I have listened my dear love! with the utmost attention to your sweet and superexcellent poem, and am so convinced of your taste and abilities that I would advise you to extend your reading through the whole circle of science and literature. Amongst other things I would recommend the study of medals, for experience has taught us that there are some medals of Herod I. surnamed the great, on one side whereof is found Ἡρωδον, and on the other Εθναρχου that is, Herod *the ethnarch*. After the battle of Philippi, we read that Anthony passing over into Syria, constituted Herod and Phasael his brother *tetrarchs*, and in that quality committed to them the administration of the affairs of Judea. Josephus

---

[32] In Mrs De Malthe's speech that follows, Beckford imitates the tediously pedantic and convoluted style of Piozzi in her book, *British Synonymy; or, An Attempt at Regulating the Choice of Words in Familiar Conversation* (1794).

indeed gives Herod the appellation of *tetrarch* instead of that of *ethnarch*; but the two terms come so near each other, that it is easy to confound them together. With regard to the word *gehenna*, which is a scripture term, and if I mistake not occurs to St Matthew, it has given the critics some pain. The authors of the Louvain and Geneva versions retain the word *gehenna* as it stands in the Greek; the like does Monsieur Simon: the English translators render it by hell and hell-fire, and so do the translators of Mons and father Bohours. The word in my opinion is formed from the Hebrew *gehinnon*, that is, valley of Hinnom. In that valley which was near Jerusalem, there was a place named *Tophet* where some Jews sacrificed their children to Moloch, by making them pass through the fire—King Josias, to render this place for ever abominable, made a cloaca or common sewer thereof, where all the filth and carcasses in the city were thrown. Now you must know, my dear! the Jews observe farther, that there was a continual fire kept up there to burn and consume those carcasses somehow; for which reason, as they had no proper term in their language to signify hell, I cannot but believe that they made use of the expression *gehenna* or *gehinnon*, to denote a fire unextinguishable. You have heard my charming dear! of the two sorts of *fasti*, the greater and the less, the former being distinguished by the appellation *fasti magistrates*, and the latter by that of *fasti kalendares*. *Fasti*, or *dies fasti*, also denoted court days. The words *fasti fastorum* are formed of the verb *fari*, to speak, because during those days, the courts were opened, causes might be heard, and the Prætor was allowed *fari*, to pronounce the three words, *do, dico, addico*: the other days wherein this was prohibited were called *nefasti*: thus Ovid

> Ille nefastus erit, per quem tria verba silentur:
> Fastus erit, per quem lege licebit agi.[33]

But I fear my charming Precious! that I fatigue you by these foolish learned allusions; you had much rather I doubt not, sweet dear! discuss the *fit* of a cap, and the fall of a flounce, because, you have so correct a taste in musick, and sing so seraphically, that you run away with all the mens' hearts, pretty love!'

'Hah!' said Miss Maleverer, smiling on Mrs. De Malthe, 'you have hit the right nail upon the head, believe me, madam!' Lucinda could not stand it, she turned away to conceal her blushes, and the Parson, pitying her embarrassment, broke up the party.

---

[33] Ovid, *Fasti*, Bk. I, ll. 47-8. 'That day is unlawful on which the three words may not be spoken/ That day is lawful on which the courts of law are open.' Translation by Sir James G. Frazer (London: Harvard University Press, 1959), 4-5.

XIX

The Beauties of Letter Writing

The sorrows of the pensive Arabella encreased every hour—she knew not where to look for consolation—all was dreary—no sunny ray to gild the distant prospect. Her Henry gone—Ah whither? Mrs. Marmaduke totally forgotten—and no news whatever from her beloved Amelia de Gonzales. The clouds of woe that inundated her afflicted heart, would never more, she feared, blossom into hope—but her chain of reasoning was now interrupted by the entrance of Margaret Grimes who presented her with a letter, and who having seated herself in an arm-chair, with her scalded leg upon a stool, listened with great attention to its contents.

To Miss Arabella Bloomville

'My dear Arabella!

A thousand thanks are due to my dearest friend for her kind kind letter. If ever I deviate from the path of duty I should be inexcusable: I write without reserve, and indeed I never harboured a thought I wish to conceal from you: no my dear Bloomville! you shall ever be the repository of my thoughts, and the guide of my actions.

I was so delighted on the receipt of your letter that I retired to my chamber to give it an attentive perusal. The gay Miss Macnamara, hearing where I was, burst into the room, 'Hey-day!' she cried, 'what but ten days in town, and have already received a love epistle as long as a law indenture? Well who is it?

Oh! answer me,
Let me not burst in ignorance '[34]

Indeed, said I, my dear Miss Macnamara, you are mistaken: this is from my Arabella. To convince her, I read some parts of it, and will send you a few of

[34] Shakespeare, *Hamlet*, I, iv, ll. 45-6.

her comments. The first general one was 'Your Arabella, child, is certainly the offspring of Jupiter's brain, I wish you would lend her letter to Mr. Danby, to take into the pulpit with him next Sunday. I'll swear he never preached so exquisite a sermon. Lord, how my head would have ached after writing so much.' My dear Arabella, said I, is fond of writing and reading, and we have, by a country life, a great deal of time for these amusements; and for my own part I must confess, though I like town for a few weeks, yet the country is my choice for constant residence. What charming walks! how pleasant to hear the whistling of birds, the bleating of sheep, and to see the people employed in rustic business.

'No more, no more,' exclaimed Miss Macnamara: 'O! defend me from being buried in the country.'

Sans *balls*, sans *plays*, sans taste, sans every thing.[35]

Take my word for it, as honest Ranger says,[36] thou art a mighty silly girl. You find I *do* read—I have read plays, child, innumerable. Romances are too long and tiresome. Novels that are full of the marvellous and surprising, I can't attend to.'

In this manner she ran on till it was time to go to the play, 'What is the play, Emily?' said she with her usual vivacity; I could not inform her—'Why, it is the Fool, written by Captain Vatass,[37] do you know the Captain?—he is an amazing *quiz*—great whiskers—no skirts. Ha ha ha!'

And when we were at the play, every gentleman who came into the box was an *ugly devil*, or a *handsome toad*; but with Sir Peter Mapletoft, the assiduous Sir Peter, she was incessantly chatting, sometimes laughing at him, at other times enquiring after every unknown face. Then ridiculing every disagreeable or unfashionable appearance with so much humour, that though I was vexed at the interruption, and could not approve her satirical talents, it was impossible to forbear laughing.

I called on her next morning, and found her playing with her monkey, and lap-dog. I asked her how she could chuse to lose time so. 'Child,' said she, with

---

[35] A comic corruption of Jaques's famous 'All the world's a stage' speech: 'Sans teeth, sans eyes, sans taste, sans everything,' in Shakespeare's *As You Like It*, II, vii, l.166.

[36] A major character in Benjamin Hoadly's *The Suspicious Husband* (1747), one of the favourite comedies of the day.

[37] A two-act farce by Major Edward Topham (1751-1820), first performed at the Theatre-Royal, Covent Garden in 1785. Topham was also the editor of a daily paper, *The World*, a favourite venue for the works of the Della Cruscans. 'Vatass' is an obvious reference to Topham's enormous *derrière*, as often featured in the many caricatures of him in satiric prints of the day, such as James Gillray's *Hyde Park; Sunday,—or—Both Hemispheres of the World in a Sweat*, published in 1789. A 'quiz' was an odd or eccentric person.

an affected gravity, 'do you understand the nature of time? Time, as Mr. Lock observes, is a succession of ideas.[38] Now, my dear, it is evident no person can have a quicker succession of ideas than I; *consequently* I can't lose time, since I enjoy its very essence, what constitutes *its existence*. Heigh ho! I have almost done tormenting the men, poor devils—I am almost married;'—'why surely,' said I, 'you are satisfied with your choice?' 'Satisfied! you little foolatum,' interrupted she, 'why to be sure, I should not have given the man such hopes of happiness, if I had preferred any other—but I had, notwithstanding, rather live single. Though, on second thoughts, I don't know what to say—he is a good-natured genteel creature enough—a simpleton, *I believe*. You are perhaps convinced of it; but no matter; many a husband is made a fool of; now my *intended* is naturally such, more reputable for me, let me tell you.'

Our conversation was here interrupted by the monkey, who having observed her playing with a beautiful dress cap, snatched it out of her hands, and pulling it with his teeth and fingers, soon rendered it unfit for use. 'O you mischievous little devil,' she cried, 'what are you about? See, Amelia! nay don't interrupt him, how prettily the toad holds the lace. My sweet pug, if it had been worth a thousand pounds, I must have laughed as I do now at thy roguery!'

She then catched him up, and in the presence of George Stapleton kissed him several times. The little animal seemed to enjoy the frolic, and looked as if he wished for another prey. I was fearful my muslin petticoat might be his next attempt, and I found Miss Macnamara did not chuse to disappoint him. I took leave sooner than I should have done, if she had been quite alone, or had had better company.

I shall expect another letter from my dear Arabella, with as much impatience as the first; and while I wish to merit her approbation, I entreat her never to spare any deserved reproof. It can be only by pursuing the advice of the best of friends, and attempting to copy the model of her example, I can become worthy of her esteem; which, with a continuance of her affection, is essentially necessary to complete the happiness of her ever affectionate friend Amelia De Gonzales.'

P.S. I yesterday was in company with the young Charles Grandison;[39] he is a wild spirited youth, and totally unlike his grandfather the celebrated Sir

---

[38] John Locke (1632-1704), the philosopher and author of *An Essay Concerning Human Understanding* (1690).

[39] A reference to the central character of Samuel Richardson's *Sir Charles Grandison*, (1753-54), designed as a male 'Pamela', a positive model of masculine behaviour in contrast to the devious and rakish male characters that appeared in his other novels.

Charles, who is still alive. He said, which made us all laugh, 'The old square toes continues to wear a full suit of gold laced cloaths, with bag and sword; he bows upon Lady Grandison's shrivelled hand twenty times in an hour, gives every body advice, and takes the air in his chariot and six.' Adieu.

Margaret Grimes being fast asleep, and Arabella herself feeling much inclined to yawn, she drew from her pocket the miniature portrait of her adorable Henry, and gazing on it with a steadfast look, fetched a deep sigh, and retired.

XX

Arabella's Embarrassment,
and the Beginning of a Voyage

Solitude is the nurse of sorrow, and therefore Arabella loved to be alone; her affection for her dear Henry every hour increased, in spite of the sly remarks of Miss Dawkins, and the artful insinuations of Miles Matthews—she was convinced that his heart was good; and though the custards were all spoiled, yet she was persuaded that Lady Fairville was innocence itself. It is not possible to separate ideas where there is prevarication, and disorders accumulate in proportion to desultory opinion. For this reason, when the star of evening began its gradual course to the antipodes, she sauntered from her cottage in that frame of mind, which disappointment naturally inculcates.

As she was elegantly leaning with her forehead against a beech tree, in the vicinity of Mr. Pasley's park, she observed a youth approach her of an interesting countenance, and engaging mien. He was dressed in a light robe of green taffety, and a bonnet of yellow sarsenet, and had in his hand a hop-pole, hung with bunches of grapes. He gazed at her with admiration and delight; then throwing himself at her feet, implored that beneficence which so singularly marked her character. As she looked at his large black eyes, a new and tender emotion took possession of her soul, and for a moment she forgot the superiority of Henry. 'Ah! Madam,' said the youth, 'if your condescension knew the agitation of my intellect, a feebler tone might suffice, but as it is, nature may pass away, before this pulse shall cease to throb with love and adoration.'

She replied with a half smile, that was inexpressibly sweet, 'Indeed, young gentleman, your behaviour entitles you to consideration and respect; your whole conduct is unexceptionably correct; but my little cottage is the abode of peace. Removed from the idle occupations of splendid greatness, and the commercial bustle of self-interest, I there devote myself to contemplation and retirement. Ah me! I am the most disconsolate of women.' Here a flood of tears came seasonably to her relief, and the youth catching her in his arms, vowed eternal constancy, and affection without end.

He instantly mounted his horse, which was a sorrel nag of considerable value, and giving the view-hollow,[40] disappeared in an instant.

Margaret Grimes had been sent to Amelia, who was just returned into the country, when the Bishop received the cheeses by the London Carrier, and consequently she had no time to enter into any discussion upon the matter. Henry, it is certain, had been twice hunting in that neighbourhood, and supped at Parson Grigsby's, with Major Ellerby and some other officers, totally unconcerned as to the result of the West-India expedition.[41] At least it appeared so by his conduct, for George Simms declared he had been thrashing all day, and had not dined when the accident happened.

When Arabella heard these strange circumstances, she was at a loss what plan to pursue; yet she thought it would be the wisest way, to pay a visit to Lady Fairville, as if nothing had happened. Taking up her pen, therefore, as usual, and bending her left knee to the ground, to give herself a greater spring, she produced the following verses.

On a Dead Goldfinch

Poor little bird that died one day,
As kings and other people may!
Ah! what would gentle Henry say
To find your life thus past away?

But Henry, O my pretty dear!
Is gone far off, and is not here.
Therefore does Arabella fear,
He is not overmuch sincere.

When next the moon begins to rise,
Again thou wilt not ope thine eyes,
And thus my faithless Henry flies,
And leaves me looking at the skies.

---

[40] i.e. a 'view-halloo' or call to the hounds.

[41] Approximately 31,000 troops were sent to the British West Indies between December 1795 and March 1796 to quell the violence of slave revolts and counter-offensive activities there on the part of the French. Michael Duffy, *Soldiers, Sugar, and Seapower The British Expeditions to the West Indies and the War against Revolutionary France* (Oxford: Clarendon Press, 1987), 196.

Begone then balmy zephyrs, go,
And let my cruel Henry know
That on this fruitful earth below,
No other man could use me so!

My Goldfinch died—how did he dare,
To leave me lost in deep despair?
Then let each maiden, sunk in care,
Of Lovers such as mine, beware.

Having relieved her anxious mind by the above soft effusion, Arabella wrote a long letter to the Countess, and offered to submit the whole matter to arbitration; she also requested the loan of her Ladyship's telescope, for the purpose, if possible, of shaming Henry out of his present pursuit; for she well knew the impossibility he laboured under of collecting fossils in that part of Lincolnshire, and rather wished to have it in his own hand writing, than through any other medium whatever.

Such was the situation of these two unfortunate lovers, and so sure was she of his fidelity, that no power on earth could have tempted her beyond the boundary of her garden, for the remainder of that week.

This precaution was however premature, for General Barton made a point of the whole party coming to the ball, and as Amelia had promised to introduce Don Pedro, who had but just arrived from Spain, so it was expected that Arabella would have sent an express to Henry, and earnestly have requested him to try the effect of the Bath waters, if the pain in his side continued.

Henry obeyed the summons with the utmost alacrity, and the wind being fair, towards evening, the vessel got out of the harbour. As the shore lessened from his view, he offered up one sigh to Love and Arabella, and then retired to his cabin in all the silent bitterness of anguish and dismay.

XXI

A Wise Lecture

Lucinda Howard now removed to the house of Mrs. Maltrever in Portman Square,[42] was introduced into all the first company in London. Her engagements were endless, and what with dinners, assemblies, and public places, she was almost harrassed out of her life, and the constant attention and invariable pursuit of Sir Sidney Walker disgusted her extremely. Mrs. Maltrever endeavoured to comfort her, and being a woman of superior understanding and uncommon penetration, one morning, after they had been to Wandsworth, in Captain Harland's phaeton, took her into a private study, and thus with emotion addressed her. 'My dear and amiable Lucinda, it is impossible for a young woman entering life, whatever may be her connections, to avoid that sort of petulance and incongruity, which is but too often the result of ill-placed ambition, and a desire to distinguish herself in literary composition. Dress, for instance, is a natural propensity, but if dispensed with too liberal a hand, degenerates by degrees into a specious kind of contumely. I was once myself a giddy girl, and at the time Mr. Maltrever fell a victim to my charms, was perhaps as fond of fields sports, as any alderman amongst them. I had been at Spa with Lady Green and her family, when I first entered upon the plan of life, which unfortunately was my chief inconvenience, for had I known the world well, I certainly should not have built this house during my husband's absence, nor should I have written those works which have impressed the public with a sense of impropriety which certainly does not belong to me. Here then lies the error of your conduct, and sorry am I to say. Miss Howard, in many instances of late, I have discovered a carelessness in your outline that totally destroys the effect of crayon painting. For the principal beauty of it consists in a certain

---

[42] Griebel makes a convincing case that Mrs Maltrever is a caricature of Elizabeth Montagu (1720-1800), noting that she built a house in Portman Square in 1781, after her husband's death, that she was such a 'giddy girl' when she was young that she was dubbed 'Fidget,' and that she had visited Spa, the Belgian resort, in 1763 as in the case of Maltrever. Griebel, 313-14. Montagu's London house was a well-known gathering place for intellectuals and social high brows. As a neighbour, Beckford attended some of the social events. In her role as 'Queen of the Blues,' she promoted female learning and achieved some celebrity for her writings, particularly for her *Essay on the Writings and Genius of Shakespear* (1769).

harmony, and an attention to general agreement, as I fear I have frequently before been obliged to observe to you.

'Now Sir Sydney Walker it must be owned, has a fine estate, and in point of family, is unexceptionable; but you know, Lucinda, that he is not in parliament, and that he goes into the North every other year to pass several weeks with Lady Fairville. On this, therefore, I shall make no comment, but you, my dear, are the best judge, how far you could be happy with a man, who has, perhaps, the finest collection of pictures in Europe, and who went to Copenhagen, to settle the herring fishery on a more permanent establishment. It is irksome, it is painful to me, to speak to you in this manner, because I know the goodness of your heart, and I am sure for my own part, I am only actuated by the interest I take in what concerns you, for I made no objection to their cutting down Hadleigh Grove, nor did I wish you to go to America, even at the time when your poor father was such a martyr to the gout. You will, therefore, no doubt, do justice to my pretensions, and in some degree, relieve me from that corroding anxiety, which has too long and too severely preyed upon my health. A love of pleasure is the bane of the youthful mind, and a too great earnestness in worldly matters, gives a tone of restlessness to most people, which, in their latter days, they cannot readily discuss with any sort of coolness, or disesteem.

Beyond the fix'd and settled rules
Of vice and virtue in our schools.[43]

'As the poet says, lies all the difference between immorality and that fatal chasm in human affairs, which tends to overcharge the brain, and disseminate erroneous opinions.—Then do not, my dear girl, mistake my motives; my only wish in life is to see you well established on a permanent foundation, that may defy the biting blasts of calumny, and avoid by its efficacy the absurdities of society in general. In the country, it is true, we escape those scenes of folly, which dislocate the capital, but there also we are subject to the ill effects of climate, and the frequent variations which the best of us cannot resist or subdue. In the intercourse with the gay and dissipated, the moral obligations subside, and reason triumphantly prevails over the wild extravagancies, which pervert the general well-being of the human race. I have now done with reproach, I am confident, my beloved Lucinda sees her own conduct in its

---

[43] Matthew Prior (1664-1721), 'Paulo Purganti and His Wife: An Honest, But Simple Pair," ll. 1-2, *The Poetical Works of Matthew Prior* (Boston, 1878), I: 134-40.

true point of view, and will not enter into any engagements, that, originating in impropriety, can only tend to tarnish the pure lustre of virtue, and to occasion that species of regret, which is irresistible in the extreme.'

Here the old lady paused, and with much seeming contrition, wiped away the falling tears, that copiously bedewed her aged cheeks, while Lucinda expressed her gratitude in the warmest terms of acknowledgement, and, actuated by the most graceful impulse, spontaneously drank her health in a bumper of Tokay, which had been sent as a present to Mrs. Maltrever, by a celebrated merchant of Hamburgh, who, during the whole war, had supplied the British navy, with indigo, cocoa nuts, and cochineal.

The door of the room now burst open with a sudden jerk, and Arabella Bloomville, with a haggard countenance and dishevelled hair, rushed in, and a moment after, fell lifeless upon the carpet. By the care and attention of Mrs. Maltrever and Lucinda, she was soon restored to some appearance of sensation, and was carried to bed by the butler, who seemed tenderly to interest himself in her recovery. In consequence of this awful event, the party was put off, the mantua-maker was dismissed, five physicians were called in to her relief, and the lap-dog was locked up in the pantry.

XXII

A Duel

At six o'clock in the morning, Don Pedro with the Chevalier de Berlingier, repaired to Kensington Gravel Pits,[44] according to appointment, where they were seen joined by Lord Mahogany and Sir Paul Danbury. The ground being measured, which was sixteen paces, Lord Mahogany asked Sir Paul if the Oxford coach was gone by; this disconcerted Don Pedro, who fired his pistol in the air, and the Chevalier leaping over the ditch, seized the bull by the horns. Lord Mahogany had climbed up a tree in the utmost consternation, but seeing the milk-woman drop upon her knees to Sir Paul, he took a pinch of snuff, and returned to the attack. He, therefore, with cool resolution and determined rage, pointed his pistol at his antagonist; but the pheasant flew away at the report of the piece, and the link boy[45] throwing a squib into his Lordship's right eye, put him off his bias, of which Don Pedro instantly took advantage; for pulling out his memorandum book, he wrote down every particular with undeniable precision. As Lord Mahogany declared he was by no means satisfied, the seconds interposed, and begged Don Pedro to consider that such a display of horsemanship at this time, was totally unnecessary. In consequence of fresh difficulties arising, Don Pedro fired, and the pigeon fell; which convinced Lord Mahogany of his mistake, and induced him so far to apologize, as to say, 'That he thought Amelia's hair of the most beautiful color, and that he would have said the same in Spain, or any other part of Europe. That as for any evil intention, he disclaimed it; he acknowledged, indeed, that he had spoken highly of Amelia's personal accomplishments, but that he actually had not proposed the party of pleasure on the water, and that if Don Pedro thought he had, he was extremely sorry for it.' The Chevalier objected to this part of the proposal; in consequence of which, they again renewed the combat. Don Pedro's pistols were Spanish, and Lord Mahogany

---

[44] The Kensington Gravel Pits were located north-west of London, at the end of Wesborn (Westbourne) Green Lane.

[45] A boy who carried a torch light to assist passengers along dark streets.

had a pair of Wogden's,[46] which having the air of an advantage of his part, he offered to bet a thousand pounds, that Sir Paul Danbury had not been present at the dinner. Don Pedro now cast a look of ineffable contempt on his Lordship, and artfully insinuated that the Lisbon Mail had been lost the preceding week; but this Lord Mahogany totally denied; so that as the matter was not likely to be otherwise accommodated, they fired a third round. Lord Mahogany having on a large cocked hat, his adversary's ball passed innocently by; but Don Pedro was not so fortunate, for his Lordship's shot struck an oak tree within twenty yards of him, thence glanced into a horse pond, and killed an old woman's pig, that was asleep in its stye.

The combatants became more furious than ever, at this juncture, their eyes flashed hatred and destruction, and Lord Mahogany with a firm tone demanded, whether Don Pedro really supposed him capable of libelling an Archbishop, who had never been guilty of one good action in the whole course of his life. This question was ill timed, for Don Pedro, foaming with fury, entreated the Chevalier to attend particularly to this last denunciation. Again therefore, with wonderful accuracy, Don Pedro discharged his pistol, and Lord Mahogany bounding three feet from the ground, pitched perpendicularly upon his toe, and spun around for some time like the flyer of a jack, then putting the little finger of his left hand into his ear, and with the other hand gracefully taking off his hat, he vociferously railed out 'God save the king.' This immediately softened the sanguinary temper of Don Pedro, who was the most loyal grandee in Spain, he flung himself into the arms of Lord Mahogany, and declaring that the dispute was now perfectly accommodated, begged that they might exchange neckcloths.

Sir Paul Danbury and the Chevalier Berlingier, waited with extreme earnestness for his lordship's reply, who drawing his sword, instantly presented it with the most engaging politeness to a barber's wife, who was opening oysters for a Scotch pedlar at the corner of the meadow.

The whole affair being thus amicably adjusted, they all entered the boat together, which glided rapidly down the stream towards the place of their destination, where the lovely and agonizing Amelia expected them, with doubt and trepidation. In their progress Don Pedro saw a bird swimming upon the surface of the water, and asked Lord Mahogany to inform him of its English appellation. His lordship answered him with wonderful readiness, by the following extemporary enigma:

---

[46] Wogden was one of the most famous duelling pistol makers in England at this time.

The fourth letter of the alphabet,
What every body is often called,
A simple sound expressive of the ocean,
And the beginning of all Kings.

Thus this tremendous day, the dew of which was so overcast, the morning of which loured so much, and came on heavily with clouds, was now changed to soft serenity, mild tranquility, sober peace, meek harmony, and concluded with general satisfaction.

XXIII

The Dangers of a Masquerade

The ladies were all in high preparation for the ensuing masquerade. Mrs. Maltrever who had visited in her early days the coast of Malabar, fixed upon the dress of a peasant of the Alps, as most suitable to her situation in life. Lucinda chose to assume the character of Queen Elizabeth, Margaret Grimes was disguised as Cardinal Wolsey, and the celestial Arabella, like a simple dairy-maid, in white sattin, with a little black feather, perking over her left ear,

Appear'd like an angel, new drop'd fron the skies.[47]

General Barton went as an old cloaths man. Sir Sydney Walker as a pair of nutcrackers, and Captain Harland as a blacksmith. When they arrived at the Theatre in the Haymarket, the gayety of the lights, the proportions of that elegant building, and the splendor of the surrounding company delighted them beyond measure. Arabella felt an unusual flow of spirits, and Lucinda whispered a blue domino[48] with particular emotion. The devil now seized Arabella by the hand, and standing upon his head drank up a whole bottle of champagne without flinching. This occasioned great merriment on both sides, and Sir Sydney being quite intoxicated, added a fresh stimulus to her vivacity. Sterne's melancholy Maria,[49] dressed in straw, now advanced with a crowd of admirers in her train; then tossing her head at sight of Arabella she said, 'well to be sure, I dare to say this *here creter* thinks herself the *biggest* beauty in the place.' Arabella no sooner heard this rude attack of the lovely maniac, than she swooned away, which threw three gentlemen into fits, and shattered the

---

[47] From a song by Thomas Parnell (1679-1718), 'When Thy Beauty Appears,' l. 3: 'All bright as an angel new dropp'd from the sky.'

[48] i. e. a blue cloak with a hood normally worn at masquerades. Sometimes, a domino would refer to the mask used for the occasion.

[49] Laurence Sterne's Maria de Moulines, a character in *Tristram Shandy* (1760-61) and in *Sentimental Journey* (1768), driven mad by being deserted by her lover and the loss of her goat.

great lustre that was suspended from the dome. This was indeed a chance, but the pathetic Maria paid little attention to the alarming confusion she had occasioned. Oh the contrary, she took her guitar and sung the following mournful elegy with such invincible pathos, that Lord Mahogany himself, who was there in the character of a milestone, burst into tears:

Elegy

Where flow meand'ring thro' the verdant plain,
    Yon rill with murm'ring melancholy flows,
Contiguous to the spot where, hapless swain!
    Young William's straw-clad cottage once arose.

Lost in incomprehensibility
    Of those dire pangs which rent his tortured breast,
When on his death-bed laid with many a sigh,
    His soul departed, leaving me unblest,

I gaily hasten'd to the well-known spot,
    Where I had oft partaken curds and tart,
Untir'd by repetition, 'twas my lot,
    To share the dainties of his dairy's art.

The slipp'ry butter which In daily course,
    Was by his pretty sister Mary made,
Ah happy days, but now distress, remorse,
    In sad perfection my torn thoughts invade.

For gone alas! are this once blissful pair,
    And anguish only now remains for me;
He left a monkey, that my griefs shall share,
    And mourn the season I no more shall see.

This beautiful effusion was received with unbounded plaudits, when Mrs. Maltrever screamed out 'O heavens! she's gone, she's gone,' at which a sailor exclaim'd 'yes, damme she's off.' This occasioned a violent burst of laughter, while Mrs. Maltrever and Lucinda fell into the orchestra, and unfortunately broke Signer Corvino's capital violoncello.

When the ladies got home, the horror of the scene is not to be described, the servants were dispatched to Pimlico and Bear-key, Mrs. Maltrever's own woman went to Billingsgate, but all in vain, no tidings of the celestial fugitive could in any manner be procured. Towards noon a lad of about eighteen, who was a brickmaker in the environs of London came to Mrs. Maltrever's house, and informed her, that being at work about five o'clock in the morning, he saw a chaise and four drive by, in which were two old ladies and a child. 'That being the case, my lady!' said he, 'I looked after them a good bit, and saw a *gelman* ride past on a grey mare, and in a brown coat, so said I to Bet, I'll be a *bobstock* of ale, if you have a mind, so she said, says she, with all my *gizzard*, now we had not been at the sow and harrow above ten minutes, before a livery servant came in for a pint of twopenny, *whereby* says I where are you going sir? Now he was a black looking man to be sure, and says he, we have lost our Miss from Mol Traver's in Portman Square, and whoever can give *count* of her shall have ten *quids*. Now my lady, I does believe, she was in the *chay* with a great squire that I seed an hour afterwards, for she was desperate pretty and screamed out mainly, so I hopes you'll give me the bounty for my *dickscovery*.' The whole company were so entertained by the lad's naiveté, that they presented him with a shilling, and all agreeing that he possessed infinite humour, advised him, if possible to get into the church; Lucinda smiled inwardly at the comicality of the idea, and vowing eternal enmity to all masquerades, took her diamond ring from her finger, and wishing Arabella all possible success, danced a Scotch reel with Lord Mongomery to the admiration of all the spectators.

Now pursuing, now retreating,
Now in airy circles meet,
To brisk notes in cadence beating,
Glance their many twinkling feet.[50]

---

[50] Slight variation of Thomas Gray's 'The Progress of Poesy A Pindaric Ode,' ll. 32-5, which reads:

Now pursuing, now retreating,
Now in circling troops they meet;
To brisk notes in cadence beating
Glance their many-twinkling feet.

XXIV

A Terrible Loss, and
a Projected Journey

Wilhelmina Countess of Fairville was the descendant of an ancient and honourable house in North Wales.[51] Her father, the Marquis of Mushroom,[52] inherited all those brave qualities and stern virtues, which had so eminently distinguished his ancestor's breed of sheep, from the cows of Spain, or the heavy beasts of the low countries. Early in life he lost a wife whom he tenderly loved, and he seemed to derive his sole consolation from playing at leap-frog with the children she had left behind. His son whom he had brought up to the arms himself so honourably bore, fell out of a back garret before he reached his nineteenth year; an elder daughter died of the whooping cough in her infancy. Wilhelmina, who had recovered from the measles, was his sole surviving child. His castle was situated in one of those delightful vallies in Wales, in which the beautiful and the sublime are so happily united; where the magnificent features of the scenery are contrasted, and their effect heightened by the blooming luxuriance of woods and pasturage, by the gentle windings of the stream, and the ruinous aspect of the falling cottages.

The Marquis was now retired from the service, grey age having overtaken him one day in an expedition to the West Indies. His residence was the resort of all foreigners of distinction, who had fled from their own country to escape the horrors of liberty, and who, attracted by the united talents of the soldier, the philosopher, and the cook, under his hospitable roof, enjoyed good beef and pudding, eels, mutton cutlets, Irish stew, and pigeon pie, besides strong beer, vegetables and pastry.

Among the visitors of this description, was the late Earl of Fairville, who was then on his travels through Wales, very much pitted with the small-pox. The

---

[51] The source for most of this chapter with variations, and excluding the two poems, was Ann Radcliffe's *The Castles of Athlin and Dunbayne: A Highland Story* (1789). Source identified by Griebel, 396-8. For actual passages, see reprint edition of 1821, New York: Arno Press, 1972, 143-9.

[52] André Parreaux suspected that the 'Marquis of Mushroom' was Walter Douglas (1725-1810), the fourth Duke of Queensbury. Parreaux, 6.

beauty of Wilhelmina, whose hair was rather sandy, embellished by a mind, highly and elegantly cultivated, touched his heart, as it were with the tip of an eagle's feather, and he instantly solicited her hand and glove in marriage.

The manly sense of the Earl, who was allowed to be the best shot in the county, and the excellencies of his disposition, had not passed unobserved, or unapproved by the Marquis or his steward, while the graces of his person, and of his mind, had anticipated for him in the heart of Wilhelmina, a pre-eminence over every church dignitary that she knew.

The Marquis of Mushroom had but one objection to the marriage, which was his hatred of leeks in general, and this was likewise the objection of Louisa, who had an equal aversion from potatoes, neither the one nor the other could endure the idea of a mode of nourishment which would be so disagreeable to them.

Wilhelmina was to the Marquis the last prop of his declining age. The Marquis was to Wilhelmina the father, the doctor, and the friend, to whom her heart had hitherto been solely devoted, and from whom it could not now be torn, but in a multiplied ratio of the unknown quantity.

This remained an insurmountable obstacle till it was removed with the garden wall by the tenderness of the Earl, who entreated the Marquis to quit North Wales, and reside with his daughter in Berkshire. The attachment of the Marquis to his natal land, and the pride of hereditary consequence, were too powerful to suffer him to acquiesce in the proposal, without a violent disorder in his bowels, and some appearance of the ague.

The desire of securing the drawings of his child, by a union with such a character as the Earl's, and of seeing her established in all her conjugal rights, before death should deprive her of the investigation of a father, at length subdued him to the lowest pitch of despondency, and he resigned the hand and seal of his daughter to the rapturous avidity of the amorous Earl.

The Marquis adjusted his affairs, and assigning his estates to the care of some old rusty agents, bade a last adieu to the landed interest, which, during sixty years, had been the principal object of his happiness, and of his regrets. The course of years had not obliterated from his heart the early affections of his youth: he took a hop-step-and-jump over that grave, which enclosed the reliques of his wife, from which it was not his least effort to depart, and whither he ordered all letters and parcels to be conveyed.

Wilhelmina quitted Wales, with a pain in her head, scarcely less acute than that of her father; the poignancy of which, however, was greatly softened down, by the tender assiduities of her lord and master, whose affectionate attentions hourly heightened her expectations, and encreased her love for the handsomest, most industrious, and best of men.

They arrived in Berkshire without any accident, where the Earl welcomed Wilhelmina, as the mistress of his domains, and immediately presented her with this delightful

Sonnet

O Wilhelmina! 'tis with double joy,
    I see thee here, both as my friend and wife,
My future hours, my dear! I will employ,
    To make thee blest, I will upon my life.

Ah! should'st thou nine months hence, produce a boy;
    To sing the cherub, I'd resume my fife,
For then my happiness could never cloy,
    And then I'd bid adieu to war and strife.

The Marquis, too, should listen to my song,
    Thy worthy father, and the best of men!
While beef and beer should cheer the peasant throng.
    But I will now a moment drop my pen,
And wait the time, for which I so much long,
    When, without fail, I'll take it up agen.

The Marquis of Mushroom had apartments in the castle, and a magic lantern to amuse him when out of spirits, and there the evening of his days declined in a very decent sort of happiness.

Before his death, he had the exquisite pleasure of seeing his race renovated in a child of the Countess, a daughter, who was a little ricketty or so, but of a clear complexion, and rather plump.

Oh the decease of the Marquis, it was necessary for the Earl to visit North Wales, in order to take possession of his estates, which, from neglect, had a good deal run to seed, and which, owing to his long absence, in many places, wanted new paleing.

He, with all his pointers, two churchwardens, and a bookseller, attended the remains of the Marquis to their last abode.

The Countess, desirous of once more beholding her young ducks and the old pigeon house, as well as anxious to pay her compliments to the memory of her Papa, entrusted her child to the care of the game-keeper, who had made her caps in her early childhood, and had accompanied the Marquis to Whitechapel on a Sunday.

Having deposited the remains of the Marquis in the coal-hole, according to his wish, and had their hair cut, they returned to Berkshire, where the first intelligence they received on their arrival at the vestry, was of the death of their daughter, and of the old game-keeper, her attendant. The poor fellow had died of the mumps, soon after their departure, the child only a fortnight before their return.

This disastrous event gave the Countess a violent creak in her neck, and afflicted the disconsolate Earl with a white swelling on his knee, and they never ceased to ridicule each other, for having entrusted their infant to a game-keeper. Time, however, subdued the poignancy of the cholic, but came fraught with another evil, more acute; this was the death of the Earl, who, in the pride of youth, with seventeen pipes of old port in his cellar, and constituting the felicity of his family, died, as he was dancing a hornpipe. He left the Countess to bewail his loss, and to wear spectacles, if ever she should attempt to read by candle light.

As soon as the Countess was arrayed in her becoming weeds, the first thought that darted across her imagination, was her much valued Lucinda Howard, to whom she immediately sent a most impressive letter, earnestly requesting her company, on a journey to Naples, which she meant instantaneously to undertake. Meanwhile, as she wished for nothing more ardently, than a fair wind to waft them across the Channel, she occupied herself in penning the following sublime and incomparable ode to Eolus, which for novelty of expression, harmony of versification, plenitude of idea, and dignity of sentiment, is not to be equalled in the English language:

Ode to Eolus[53]

O Thou! to whom great Jove[54] assign'd
The empire of each stubborn wind
    And bade them own thy sway;
'Tis thou who giv'st them leave to rage,
Thy voice their fury can assuage,
    And check their headlong way.

When Juno,[55] Heaven's imperial Dame,
A suppliant at thy feet became.

---

[53] The God of the Winds, according to the accounts given by Heathen poets. [Beckford's note].

[54] A Pagan Deity, and the first of all the Gods. [Beckford's note].

[55] A Pagan Deity, wife and sister to Jupiter. [Beckford's note].

Thou didst admit her pray'r;
For her the surges lash'd the shore,
For her thou bad'st the tempest roar
Wide thro' the troubled air.

But now a nymph whose matchless mien
Surpasses that of Jove's proud queen
Is venturing, on the deep;
O then each adverse wind restrain,
Let favouring zephyrs skim the train,
And hush the storms to sleep!

Love at the helm shall take his stand,
And guide the bark with skillful hand
Along the watry way,
The cestus which adorn'd her waist,
By Venus[56] on the topmast plac'd,
Shall like a pendant play.

Their green locks dripping briny dew,
The Nereids[57] rising to the view,
Shall each gay art employ,
And Ocean,[58] conscious of his freight,
Proud to subside beneath her weight,[59]
Soft murmuring tell his joy!

The beautiful Countess Dowager had strained her left leg so much in the composition of the above harmonious and affecting ode, that she ate a plate of prawns, drank a pot of porter, and retired to bed, agitated in the extreme.

END OF THE FIRST VOLUME

---

[56] The Goddess of Beauty, and wife of Vulcan, who used to wear a cestus. [Beckford's note].

[57] Pagan mermaids, who live in the salt sea. [Beckford's note].

[58] Alias Neptune, who is always proud on such occasions, being King of the sea. [Beckford's note].

[59] She was a very bulky woman. [Beckford's note].

MUM!

Engraved print published December 3rd, 1795 by W. O'Keeff, from the Nicholas K. Robinson Collection, courtesy of the Board of Trinity College Dublin.

MODERN NOVEL WRITING,
OR THE ELEGANT ENTHUSIAST

VOLUME II

I

An Important Discovery

After a journey of much fatigue and unpleasant rumination, Lucinda Howard, accompanied by the melodious Arabella, arrived at the Countess's elegant abode.[60] They were shewn into the drawing room, the walls of which her Ladyship had spent two years and a half in ornamenting with her own dear hands. It was entirely painted over with birds, beasts, fishes, urns, flowerpots, and arabesque figures in a most astonishing manner, so that the praises for her ingenuity, and for the laudable occupation of her time, was a constant source of vanity to her Ladyship, and a ready subject of conversation to all her visitors. But alas; the Countess, since the expediting her letter, had endured a state of dreadful suspence, although Mrs. de Malthe in friendship had endeavoured to soothe her Ladyship's distress, by her constant presence, and the most unbounded admiration of the pictures and pier glasses, and particularly the curtains. She was entering into an elaborate treatise on taste, when the noise of horses at the gate reached her ears. 'It is my Lucinda,' said Mrs. de Malthe, rising from her chair, 'It is my dear Lucinda, she brings us life or death.' She said no more, but winking at Captain Harland, and with a comical snap of her fingers, rushed forwards, and with an oval movement, clasped the almost expiring Lucinda to her bosom. The transport of the scene repelled utterance; sobs, tears, and chocolate drops, were all that could be given. Let those who have experienced such superabundant bliss, declare, how inconceivably gratifying are the encomiums of virtue, when softened by the breezes of content.

The general joy, however, was suddenly dissipated by the Countess, who fell senseless to the floor; delight yielded to surprise, and to the business of assistance. On recovering, the Countess looked wildly round her, and Doctor Philbert took a cup of coffee. This giving the whole company breathing time, Lord Damplin objected to the manœuvre, and her Ladyship exclaimed, 'Was it a vision that I saw, or a reality?' Every body put on their spectacles, but could not discover any

---

[60] The source for most of this chapter up to the 'Song' was Radcliffe, *The Castle of Athlin and Dunbayne*, 273-9. Griebel, 398-9.

thing extraordinary. 'It was Mr. Bloomville himself, my first husband, his very hair, his features, under a female form; that benign countenance which I have so often contemplated in imagination.' Her fine eyes still seemed in search of some ideal object, and they began to doubt whether a sudden frenzy had not seized her brain. 'Ah! again!' said she, and instantly relapsed, with an engaging motion of her head. Their eyes were now turned towards Arabella, who was bringing a glass of water for the Countess's parrot, and on *her* the attention of all present was now centered. She approached, ignorant of what had happened, and her surprise was great, when the Countess, reviving, fixed her eyes mournfully upon her, and asked her to take off her glove. 'It is,—it is my Arabella!' said she, with a strong emotion; 'I have, indeed, found my long lost child; that strawberry on her arm confirms the decision.' The whole company crowded round them, and Jack Deeply crammed his hankerchief in his mouth. Arabella fell at the feet of her new Mamma, and bathed her hand with tears. 'Gracious me! for what have I been reserved!' She could say no more. The Countess raised, and pressed her to her heart. It was upwards of seven minutes and a half, before either of them could speak, and all present were too much affected to interrupt the silence. At length the Countess gazing tenderly upon Arabella said 'My beloved girl, within these last fifteen months, I have taught myself German.' 'Aye,' cried Doctor Philbert, 'the man who can be insensible to the charms of virtue, must be a bad moral character, and viciously inclined.' Arabella wept silently upon the neck of her mamma, while Jack Deepley exclaimed, 'Well, Poll, what have you got to say to all this?' The bird looked up archly and replied 'What's o'clock.' This gave a turn to the conversation, and fortunate indeed it was for poor Mrs. de Malthe, whose emotions almost overcame her, and were too powerful for utterance.

The company now adjourned to the cedar parlour, and Arabella withdrew to take that repose she so much required. She was sufficiently recovered in a few hours to join her friends in the green-house.

After they had eat up the ice cream, and washed their faces in vinegar, the transports of the scene became a little more calm. 'I have much to hope, and much to fear,' said Lord Damplin, taking off his coat, and jerking his hat out of the window, 'You, Madam,' addressing the Countess, 'you will willingly undertake to be my advocate with her whom I have so long and so ardently adored.' 'What, are we going to have a funeral,' cried Jack Deepley, 'that your Lordship wants the Countess to be an undertaker?' This remark occasioned a roar of laughter, but his Lordship looking very serious thus continued, 'May I hope,' taking tenderly the hand of Arabella, who stood trembling by, 'May I hope, that you have not been insensible to my long attachment, and that you will confirm the happiness which is now offered me?' A smile of ineffable sweetness broke through the melancholy which had long clouded her angelic features, and which

even the present discovery had not been able entirely to dissipate; then lightly
scratching her back with the end of her fan, and heaving a profound sigh, she thus
replied, 'No, my Lord, I never can be yours, my affections are engaged to another
gentleman, and I will never bestow my hand, where I cannot give my heart.' This
answer, so sentimental and so new, charmed the attentive audience; his Lordship
was not equal to the shock, but bursting into a flood of tears, declared, that had
he suspected matters would have turned out so, he would certainly have gone to
the boxing match, which was to be on that day at Rumford, between Johnson
and the Jew.[61]

The discourse for the remainder of the day, was occupied by the subject
of the discovery, and by a recital of Arabella's adventures, during which Jack
Deepley would frequently entertain the company with some facetious remarks
on the crest-fallen lover. He called him a suspirating senator, a perplexed peer,
a lordly lollypop, a neglected nobleman, and a love-sick legislator in hereditary
hopelessness. These lively sallies restored the good humour of the company,
and induced the amiable Lucinda to favor them with the following

Song

What is this sentimental love—
    This spell of the romantic mind,
Whose flimsy texture fancy wove
    Too weak th' impassion'd heart to bind!

Does it from nature spring? Ah! no;
    Nature the airy form denies—
Is it by reason bred? If so,
    Why always hid from reason's eyes?

Is it a quick inspiring flame
    That animates with love the *heart*?
No—its cold dictates strangely aim
    A mental fervour to impart.

---

[61] i. e. the bare-knuckle boxers, Tom Johnson (1750-1797) and the English-Jewish prizefighter Daniel
Mendoza (1764-1836). Johnson was champion from 1784 to 1791 but lost his title in a fight arranged by
Douglas, the 8th Duke of Hamilton (1756-1799) with Benjamin Brain (1753-1794). The Duke, a boxing
aficionado, was a patron of Brain. Johnson never fought Mendoza but did spark a controversy in England
when, serving as a second for Richard Humphries during a battle between Humphries and Mendoza,
he stepped in and blocked a blow from Mendoza that would have given him a decisive victory. Henry
Downes Miles, *Pugilistica The History of British Boxing*, I (Edinburgh, 1906): 63; 87

Dull apathy, or frozen age,
  The phantom conjur'd first to view,
The policy or envious rage
  Of those who ne'er true rapture knew.

Away! no more my thoughts detain,
  Illusive, visionary sprite!
May love's war stream thro' ev'ry vein
  Roll gay desire and fond delight.

And may the youth whose sparkling eyes
  For love and mutual bliss were sent,
Ne'er damp my ardours as they rise,
  With the chill clouds of sentiment.

Every body testified the highest approbation of Lucinda's voice, and exquisite mode of singing—but Mrs. de Malthe objected to the words, as having too much meaning in them to please persons of fashion, and the Countess herself glancing her eyes upwards exclaimed—'Well Miss Howard! indeed I wonder at you.' This observation set the diffident Lucinda a crying ready to break her heart, which Major Pemberton observing, he slyly looked at Jack Deepley and said 'you see, my dear boy! we are up to you.' The gloom of the moment was consequently dispersed, as the heavy vapours of morning fly before the beams of the sun.

On account of this happy discovery the Countess ordered her house to be thrown open; mirth and festivity resounded through the walls; and the evening closed by a plentiful supper given to all her Ladyship's tradespeople, who, to promote gaiety, were arranged at a long table in the servant's hall, in alphabetical order as follows: an attorney, a baker, a cheesemonger, a dustman, an engraver, a fishwoman, a grocer, a haberdasher, an informer, a joiner, a kitchen-maid, a lapidary, a mercer, a nightman, an optician, a poulterer, a quack, a reviewer, a silversmith, a taylor, a vintner, an undertaker, a writing-master, an xciseman, a yeoman, and a Zealander, who had emigrated with the Stadtholder from Holland,[62] and was a maker of Dutch tiles. Thus ended the most brilliant and blissful day the Countess had experienced for many months; a day which will long be remembered by all the guests, for Arabella's restoration to happiness, and for the hospitality, and dignified affability of her ladyship's own woman.

---

[62] Stadholder, a title for the chief magistrate of the Dutch Republic. Beckford is referring to William V, Prince of Orange who fled to England in 1795, when the French army invaded the Netherlands.

II

A Lord in Tribulation

The next morning the whole party set off to pay a visit to Arabella's humble cottage, where the watchful Margaret Grimes regaled them with apple dumplings and a syllabub, to the unspeakable satisfaction of little Master Burton, and Sophy Warley.

While they were here engaged in an instructive conversation, two rustics of the neighbourhood, knocked at the door for admittance; they supported between them, on a hurdle, a gentleman in great apparent agony. They stated they had found him in a wood, writhing under a tree; that he had implored their charitable aid, and they thought the greatest kindness they could render him, would be to bring him to that place. Arabella's humanity would not permit her to refuse any assistance she could render to a person under such circumstances. She was making the necessary arrangements for that purpose, when Amelia entered, and, with a loud shriek, announced her recognition of Lord Mahogany.

He had returned into the country the very day Lucinda had arrived at the Countess's, and had received the letter Amelia left for him; but the servant informing him from whom it came, he had thrust it carelessly into his pocket unopened, saying, he was engaged in matters of greater import, and could not attend to her messages.

La Contessa Negri had enquired for her foot-boy in the morning, and hearing he had absconded, readily conjectured the reason, though being totally unacquainted with Amelia, she could not suppose her to have any hand in the business, as Arabella very properly remarked, when the circumstance was mentioned. Well, this Italian Signora, who was deeply enamoured of Lord Mahogany, fancying that her former project might be discovered, determined, if his Lordship put himself again in her power, to trust to no other hand, but perpetrate her intention herself, and cursed her timidity, which had so far disabled her resolution and better judgment, as to make her trust such a matter to a silly boy. If Lord Mahogany, on his first visit, discovered any fear or suspicion of her, she resolved to anticipate the event of a second, by going immediately abroad; for which purpose, she packed up her jewels and money, and made all necessary arrangements; and if he fell into the snare, she thought a very short time, and a few seasonable donations, would prevent all enquiry.

Little did the Signora imagine, while she walked in the garden, that the very fate she prepared for him, was, by a counterplot, of which she could have no possible notion, impending over her own head.

In a mind, hardened by successful practice, in a course of iniquity, no scruple intruded itself to prevent the adoption of the most nefarious ones; Lord Mahogany, therefore, resolved to poison La Contessa; and to prevent all suspicion of a musical tendency, gave the answer he did to the servant, and introduced himself into her house by a private way, known and open to himself alone.

The maids and the shoe-boy were playing at blindman's buff, as he passed the Brewhouse, yet he entered carelessly into the apartment of La Contessa, eating some conserves, of which he held a box in his left hand. After the ordinary salutations, and kissing the back of her neck, he asked her to partake of his sweetmeats, which she did chearfully, foreseeing it would be a reason for her offering him some wine, in which she had infused the fatal venom.

La Contessa, overjoyed at the prospect of success, ate the conserves with avidity, and those which he took care to give her were poisoned, then immediately complaining of thirst, filled two large glasses with wine, and presented one to his Lordship which he drank off without hesitation. Thus perfectly satisfied with the event, he went away, but first he borrowed an umbrella of the coachman, because he had promised to meet General Barton at the bowling green that they might crack a bottle together, and talk over old stories.

Both La Contessa and Lord Mahogany, from an excessive solicitude to avoid suspicion, had given a poison which would not operate for some days. His lordship therefore resolved to employ the interval in travelling, and set out immediately, without its being known that he had visited La Contessa.

On the fourth day, as he was riding alone, having sent his servants forward by the waggon, and his books in the stage coach; he happened to put his hand into his pocket, and drew out the letter, which Amelia had sent him, and for want of something else to do, opened and read it.

Language is inadequate, nor would the best wrought similies afford sufficient assistance, to describe the surprize, horror, and regret, which seized him on the perusal of this paper, in which his projected murder was so far described, that his Lordship could not help feeling he had fallen a victim to the treachery of another, at the very moment he was rejoicing in the success of his own. He spurred his horse forward that he might get to some place to procure relief, but the violence of this exercise accelerated the effects of the venom. He felt parched with fever; a cruel pain seized his bowels; his eyes seemed burning in their sockets; and his strength began to fail him, so that he was obliged to dismount, and lean against a stile, he then took out his pencil and some asses skin, and in a short time composed the following illegitimate sonnet[63] without rhime:

To the Lark

Hail lofty Pindar [64] of the feather'd choir!
Whether at heaven's blest gate, on mattin wing,
Soaring thou warblest, when young Maï [65] first
Pours forth the gay luxuriance of her dies,
And hill and valley smile with sudden bloom.

Whether blithe soaring o'er the warring field,
Where bounteous Ceres [66] pours forth all her store,
Veiling glad nature's form in living gold,[67]
Thy pipe, unfailing, roves thro' ev'ry change,
Lofty or *softy*, melody divine!

Or whether, 'scaping from the fatal tube,
What time the plunder'd stubble dusky mourns,[68]
Still attic songster! [69] to the list'ning soul
Thy strains shall warble gratitude and love.

---

[63] An allusion to the debate in the 1780s and 90s over legitimate (Petrachan) versus illegitimate (Shakespearian) sonnets following the publication of Charlotte Smith's *Elegiac Sonnets* (1784). Her sonnet consisted of three elegiac quatrains and a couplet and is generally believed to have played an important role in the revival of the sonnet genre in the Romantic period. Raymond D. Havens, *The Influence of Milton on English Poetry* (New York: Russell & Russell, 1961), 503.

[64] Pindar was called the Theban Eagle, and therefore very like a Lark. [Beckford's note]. Pindar was a native of Thebes and often compared himself to an eagle. See Gray's 'The Progress of Poesy', III. 3, l. 115.

[65] Some affected poetasters of the present day have called her Maia, but surely Maï is much more agreeable to the ear. [Beckford's note].

[66] Ceres, the goddess of corn. [Beckford's note].

[67] The most malignant critic will hardly deny this line to have sublimity. [Beckford's note].

[68] Though this verse may be totally unintelligible to the vulgar, it may, perhaps, not be deemed the less beautiful by persons of taste. [Beckford's note].

[69] The Nightingale and the Owl have been hitherto called the attic birds, but surely the term is more appropriate to the Lark, which sings up aloft, i.e. in the attic story of the skies. [Beckford's note]

This sonnet, which his Lordship wrote without rime or reason, may, perhaps, be best excused by the lamentable situation in which he found himself. He had scarcely finished it, when he fell at the foot of a tree, where the clowns discovered him, and brought him to the retreat of Arabella.

III

A Digression on Patriotism,
and a Stag Hunt

'I wish,' said Lord Charles Oakley, as he came out of Covent Garden Theatre, 'I wish I knew for certain whether or no Lucinda Howard is with my mother at Fairy Lodge.' 'Why so' replied Colonel Birch, 'are you one of her admirers?' 'Faith Frank' returned Lord Charles, 'I can but little bear joking upon that head: though I am a profligate dog, to all appearance, yet the remnants of virtue still actuate a heart, too deeply interested in the peace and welfare of mankind to conform to all the current prejudices of the world.' 'Why, how now! my lord! surely you are not a democrat? what say you, shall we go to orator Gabble's political lectures,[70] he *preaches* to night, *pro bono publico,* come along Citizen[71] Oakley.' 'You *may* laugh, yet the title of Citizen is as respectable to my ears, as Lord, or any other that folly may have invented, but talk not to me of the orator and his lectures, I am only attached to principles; I hate an egotist in every situation, whatever may be his professions; nay, believe me, when I see a man putting himself forward as the *greatest* sufferer in the cause of liberty, as its *best* friend, as its *firmest* support, when he harangues a gaping multitude with an air of the *utmost importance*, tells them all the wrongs they endure, and exaggerates if possible all the oppressions they labour under, and at the same time entreats them to be orderly, patient, and submissive—when I hear and see this, Frank, I say the man cannot be sincere.' 'Why in truth,' returned the Colonel, 'if a friend was to come and tell me that Mr. Smith had called me a coward and a scoundrel, and afterwards request me to behave kindly and civilly to the said Mr. Smith, I should think my friend to be either a fool or a madman, or an imposter.' 'Besides Frank,' continued Lord Charles, 'a true patriot can have neither vanity, nor

---

[70] Very likely John Thelwall (1764-1834), the radical political orator, a key figure in the parliamentary reform movement in England during the 1790s. He was recognized as the principal orator of the London Corresponding Society, speaking regularly to large audiences, sometimes as many as 150,000, about the oppressive policies of William Pitt (1759-1806) and the government. Charles Cestre, John *Thelwall A Pioneer of Democracy and Social Reform in England During the French Revolution* (London, 1906), 121.

[71] Used here in the political sense of being a supporter of democratic principles and the French revolution.

ostentation, nor ambition, his only motive to exert himself is philanthropy, his only object, to meliorate the wretched condition of the majority of the human race. If he discover weakness or absurdity in any fellow-labourers in the vineyard he will endeavour to gloss over their errors, and not hold them up to contempt, he will feel indignation only against unblushing tyranny, and selfish assumption: but is this the case with Gabble? No—if his dearest friend were to gain more applause than he did for public speaking, that instant he would look upon him as a rival and treat him as an enemy.—Does a writer in support of freedom and truth either in prose or verse obtain any degree of popular consideration? the rancour, the jealousy of Gabble immediately burst out against him, he will attack him with a malignant, though feeble ridicule, with a virulent though inefficacious criticism, and hate him more sincerely than he does either Pitt, Dundas, Windham, Mansfield,[72] or even all of them together. Like Pantagruel he thinks to cover a whole nation with his tongue[73]—In short, this vain orator reminds me in a slight degree, *parvis componere magna*, of Robespierre,[74] who strenuously employed the energies of France, opposed its external enemies, and wished to overthrow all the tyrants of Europe, that he might remain the sole hero of the piece, and be stiled MAXIMILIAN THE FIRST, GREAT PATRIOT OF THE WORLD. 'Why you grow warm Charles,' said the Colonel, laughing, 'what say you to a couple of fine girls and a dozen of Champagne?' Here an Irish chairman interrupted their discourse, by informing them, that they had better be upon their guard and not talk sedition, for that there was a *blind* man walking under the Piazza, whom he suspected to be a *spy*.

In consequence of this intelligence, the orange-woman dropped the Courier,[75] and first asking the Hackney coachman's leave, finished the tankard

---

[72] All three of the following individuals were key members of Pitt's government: Henry Dundas, Viscount Melville (1742-1811), Privy Councillor and Treasurer of the Navy, 1784-1800 and Secretary of State for War, 1794-1801; William Windham (1750-1810), Cabinet member and Secretary at War, 1794-1801; David Murray, Earl of Mansfield and Viscount Stormont (1727-1796), President of the Council, 1794-1796.

[73] An allusion to François Rabelais's *Pantagruel*. Chapter 2, xxxii, is devoted to how Pantagruel covered a whole army with his tongue.

[74] Maximilien Robespierre (1758-1794), one of the most influential leaders of the French Revolution and a major exponent of the Reign of Terror. Following many successful political manoeuvres, he was elected president of the National Convention and served during the period 1793-4. As a powerful member of the Committee of Public Safety, he was able to exercise dictatorial authority of a revolutionary government. In a dramatic reversal, he was accused of tyranny and executed in July 1794.

[75] *The Courier*, an opposition newspaper and critic of Pitt's administration, founded in 1792. Lucyle Werkmeister, *A Newspaper History of England* (Lincoln: University of Nebraska Press, 1967), 116-17.

of porter at one draught—which so provoked a pastry-cook, who wanted to sell Lord Charles a couple of razors, that he took no notice of the Colonel, which was the more extraordinary, as the market was beginning to fill, and one of the watchmen had fallen down in an apoplexy.

They both mounted their horses with great eagerness, and though the stag took to the North, and led them a chace of five hours, and though his most sacred majesty was not present, which took much from the pleasure and interest of the day, yet they got set down to dinner, at Parson Hornby's before dark. The dove-house having been destroyed in their absence, there could be no fishing that evening; so Lord Charles drank a large bumper of brandy to the health of his favourite Lucinda Howard, and was pledged by the Colonel, in a pint of old port.

As their hopes and wishes were now deferred till the morrow, they just treated the Parson with a few jovial songs, and were carried up to bed by the house-maid, at half past two in the morning.

IV

Phrenzy, Despair, and Death

Lord Mahogany, when he was brought to the abode of Arabella, was in a state of insensibility. The violence of his agitations had exhausted him; but as soon as General Barton was informed of his situation, he prepared a decoction of simples,[76] which he said, would, if the poison was not very strong, or had not been long taken, operate as an antidote, but would, at all events, restore his reason and quiet. This was administered, and soon produced a return of sense in his Lordship: he opened his eyes, and staring wildly at the General, exclaimed with a shriek of agony—

'I am not dead. Why art thou come to torment me before my time? I know thee well; thou art an elephant.—Hah! how he handles the cards—help, help—my poor pig is in convulsions—how the tree laughs—the duck whispering that bishop is La Contessa Negri—see, see! they make bulrushes of her hair—Torment me not—I did not kill her!'[77]

General Barton was so astonished, that for some moments he could not speak; but, at length, he told Lord Mahogany, he was mistaken, and that *he* was endeavouring to do him all the services that lay in his power.

'Forgive me, holy man! forgive me,' said his Lordship. 'I am a wretch! I have thrown away a jewel! I'll give a hundred guineas for a silver muffin! what a storm it blows! and the mule speaks Greek! can you dig up the world? had I met her in the grave, for she has sweet lips, perhaps—I might have given my vote for peace! but O! 'twas war, war, war! how they bleed! thousands, ten thousands dead! such a waste of murder! bring the wheel barrow! for I will fly to Naples.' Here a tear or two rolled down his glowing cheek, and seemed to relieve him. He recollected himself, and in a composed tone of voice, said, 'I know not where I am; my ideas wander! is this my head? look! the warming

---

[76] A concoction of herbs or plants used for medicinal purposes.

[77] André Parreaux suggested that Lord Mahogany's 'fits of delirium' may be a caricature of George III's 'intermittent madness' (Parreaux, p. 4). The king had by this time suffered two mental breakdowns, one in 1765 and another in 1788. His behaviour was marked by incessant and incoherent ramblings followed by periods of lucidity, as in the case of Lord Mahogany.

pan is on fire! Is there any body will go for me to Wapping, and bring me a bason full of stockings?'

General Barton answered, 'there is.'

'Will he be faithful?' asked Lord Mahogany.

'I will be responsible for him with my life, he is a brother fox-hunter,' said the General. 'Give him these keys,' said his Lordship. And then describing, very minutely, every place, directed him to a particular part of the garden, where he would find a well, which he requested might be brought him without delay, as his life depended on it.

Amelia now entered the room. Her presence calmed and relieved him more than any other thing could have done. He called her to his bedside, and entreated her to sit, and stay with him while the General left the chamber.

'My dear woman,' said he, 'had you but lighted the fire in time, we might have gone to Banbury in a nut-shell—but O! this cursed war—I voted for it—how it burns my brain. Bring me a feather, for I would fain speak a word to the pigeon house.'

His delirium now returned, and Amelia was obliged to call in the General, who restored him to a state of quiet, by a further dose of the decoction; but this was not easily effected, and he entertained no hopes of his recovery.

Lord Mahogany, when he came to himself again, desired every one to leave the room except Amelia, he declared he could not bear to look at the features of any other person, as they all inspired him with gloomy recollections. He implored her to watch with him that night, and urged this point so earnestly, that she was obliged to submit, though not by any means fond of the employment.

The bed the miserable Peer occupied, was that where Margaret Grimes had lain the night before. General Barton and Major Pemberton sat up till a late hour, playing at backgammon; while Arabella resolved to render her patient every assistance in her power.

Lord Mahogany slept for some hours, but the little strength he gained by this refreshment heightened his fever, and when he awoke he raved with more violence than before. Amelia was obliged to call for assistance, as he threatened the most dreadful vengeance on himself. These fits of delirium supplied him with such amazing force, that the united efforts of the General and Major Pemberton could hardly keep him in bed.

'Ah!' he would exclaim, 'look how fiercely the faggots blaze—O! conscience, conscience!—the troops march—alas!—the war is mine—and the sight of that collyflower breaks my heart-strings. Do you imagine I am blind? He stands by the curtains of my bed, and asks me to buy a ferret. Ah! that's a serious question. Look at the blooming bride; she is watching the flames, with her nose in a gallipot[78]—now she is going off—see, in what agony she dies; but she did not go to war—she was a grasshopper.'

Lord Mahogany now appeared more easy, and took some refreshment from the hands of the gentle Arabella. But this transient calm was only the forerunner of a more violent storm. His phrenzy returned, and before proper help could be procured, he had jumped out of bed, and bruised himself dreadfully against the walls of the room—'To drive away,' as he said, 'a salamander that was playing on the harpsichord; look,' cried he, 'look at that pelican, how it smiles upon the imps of darkness—they chain the sun to a coal-tub—what a world it is, who can tell but it may be given to me, for my library is full of jackals, and virtue is a mere carpet—murder, war, murder cannot go unpunished.'

In this manner he continued to rave at different periods, till he grew more weak, and life seemed to ebb apace. His recollection was better, but his horrors of mind were more shocking than were before witnessed. He would not be a moment alone, and at night could not rest without three or four persons about him. The slightest noise terrified him, and he would sometimes cry out 'What is that? surely I saw a lady-bird undraw my curtains.—No, it could not be, for she was without her mackarel.' Then he would sigh deeply. He slept but a little in the night; if he did for a few minutes, he would start, and wake in the greatest agonies, and relate the most hideous and unconnected dreams.

The return of morning presented a certainty, that he could not long survive. His tongue and lips were parched and dry, spite of his frequent recourse to decoctions of General Barton's preparing. The surface of his skin exhibited a leprous appearance, and his eyes wild, glowing and deep sunk in his head, glared dismally on all around. 'Let me measure the moon,' said he, ''tis full of marrow, faugh! but O this torrent of lobsters—stop them, they curl the Heavens. Bottle up the war in a corn-field, and put my vote in hell. Hold me—the room is in flames, and the castle totters, what a serpent is the minister,[79] he has stung mankind—I am a crocodile.' He now caught hold of the bed cloaths, as if to save himself, and giving a dreadful shriek, EXPIRED.

Major Pemberton was much disconcerted at the suddenness of the event, as it prevented his going out a shooting. The rest of the company walked forth upon the terrace to vent their reflections on the extraordinary events they had witnessed, and in the evening there was a concert.

---

[78] A glazed pot used by apothecaries for ointments and medicines.

[79] i.e. William Pitt

V

Variety of Singular Events

It is a task by no means easy, to develope the workings of the human heart in all its progressive motions, yet surely the most interesting endeavour is, to divulge the perversion of the passions, and to hold out a beacon to misguided men, which shall controul the irregularities of fancy, and hourly generate the voice of wisdom, the dignity of virtue, and the incomprehensibility of shame.

Henry Lambert, seduced by the gay dissipation of the metropolis, soon launched out into every fashionable folly and extravagance; he associated with the Toms the Charleses and the Georges who exhibited their elegant persons in Bond Street every day, he became a member of the first clubs, drove a *vastly neat* curricle, and nodded familiarity to every woman of the town whether he knew her or not. He had also the credit of an intrigue with a Duchess. He was, (what is called) in a good stile. One day as he was riding carelessly in Hyde park, he observed a beautiful young woman selling nuts to an old cloaths man; he was so much struck by her appearance, that he immediately set spurs to his horse and taking off his hat with a respectful air, saluted Mrs. Wallingford, (who was just then passing in a low phaeton) as follows. 'It is a charming day ma'am, I think the air is wonderfully mild for the season.' 'Quite so indeed,' replied the Lady, 'but dear Harry! where have you been? Lady Sambrook's party was extremely dull last night, can you guess why I thought so?' 'Haven't an idea, upon my word, what can you allude to.' 'O you sly man, to pretend ignorance—I have a great mind not to tell you; shall I tell you. Harry?' 'You will oblige me infinitely, you don't know how much you'll oblige me, you can't conceive the obligation I should think it—can the finest woman in England be so hard-hearted?' 'O you monster, O you flatterer, do you know that you now make me really angry—and so you can't guess? well, however I won't tell you.' 'Yes do now, have compassion upon me, tell me why you thought it dull, pray do.' 'And so you absolutely have not the smallest notion what could be the cause of my thinking it dull.'—'Upon my credit, have not any conception of what it can be.' 'I'd lay fifty guineas,' continued the Lady, 'that in your heart, you are perfectly convinced of what

I mean.' 'No, indeed, I am upon my *parole*, I cannot discover the reason why you thought it dull last night—I am entirely at a loss.' 'Well you may protest, but I don't believe you—however, not to tantalize you, the only reason why I thought it dull last night at Lady Sambrook's was—I think I had better keep it to myself—was—now I will not say a word more about it.' 'How can you be so severe upon me?—Have mercy, my sweet woman, I shall die if you don't tell me.' 'Well then the truth shall out, I thought it dull at Lady Sambrook's for no other reason but,—O you wretch!—because *you* were not there. Now are you satisfied?'

Henry professed himself in raptures at this discovery, and instantly standing with one foot upon the saddle, set off full speed, till he reached the Serpentine river, when plunging in, he swam his horse to the opposite shore, then took a flying leap over the wall on the Uxbridge road, crossed the fields till he came near Harrow, turned to the left, and in half an hour found himself by Windsor—thence he bent his course to Henley, and reached Banbury at the very moment Major Pemberton had his tooth drawn. The soup was not yet taken away, so that Henry had just time to wash his hands, and to enquire with a faultering tone, 'how is the divine Arabella?'

The Curtain at Drury Lane Theatre had been up some time, and the great Kemble, was in the very act of being superior to Garrick,[80] when Henry Lambert entered the stage box covered with dust, and looking dreadfully fatigued. As the house was uncommonly crowded, and as a butcher from Leaden-hall Market was in hysterics in the center of the pit, so Henry did not discover Lady Fairville till towards the conclusion of the fourth act. She saw Henry with a smile of complacency, being fully convinced of the sincerity of his passion. She therefore advanced to the front of the box,[81] tall, admirably proportioned, and with a dignity of carriage peculiar to herself. A loose circassian dress of gold muslin served just to give an idea of the outline of her perfect form, her snowy arms were bare to within an inch of her shoulders, a girdle of diamonds marked the situation of her swelling bosom, and her fine brown hair fell in profusion far below her middle. A plume of ostrich, less white than her skin, rose from her forehead in lofty pride, and in the midst stood a heron's feather triumphant. A *couche* of Paris *rouge*, appeared

---

[80] John Kemble (1757-1823), prominent actor, noted for his Shakespearian tragedies, and director of the Drury Lane Theatre at this time; David Garrick (1717-1779), the celebrated actor who preceded Kemble at Drury Lane.

[81] The remainder of this paragraph was derived from *Melissa and Marcia; or the Sisters: A Novel* (London: W. Lane, 1788), I: 138-41, by Elizabeth Hervey (1759-1824), Beckford's half-sister. Source identified by Griebel, 400.

upon those cheeks, whose natural bloom required no such aid, yet it must be owned, her eyes from this circumstance received additional brilliancy, though their lustre was somewhat tempered by the dark fringe that surrounded them. Her eyebrows too were as charming as her eyes, they were much darker than her hair, and nature had pencilled them with such peculiar exactness, they needed not the aid of art. Her nose—it was not perfect—it had however as good pretensions to please as that *petit né retroussé* which overthrew the laws of a potent empire. Two ruby lips occasionally opened to shew the finest teeth in the world; and her chin, and the turn of her face were more pleasing than can be imagined: her royal highness the Duchess of York's shoemaker had the honour of making her Ladyship's shoes, and her foot was still less, if possible, and more to be admired than even that of the incomparable Princess.[82] Add to all these charms, the vivacity of forty, the self complacency that dwells on the countenance of a beauty, on the scene of her triumph; the little airs and graces of a coquette, embellished with her lover's presence; picture to yourself all this, and you will see Lady Fairville gaining the admiration of the whole audience, and gradually effacing from the mind of Henry those unfavourable impressions which Arabella's dissertation had occasioned.

Her Ladyship got through the crowd with the greatest difficulty, and did not reach her own house till two o'clock in the morning, when throwing herself upon a marble hearth before the fire, she poured forth a deluge of tears, and declared to Mrs. Marmalade, her own woman, that she was the most miserable creature upon earth.

Henry, on the contrary, passed the night in deep play, and having won fourteen hundred and sixty guineas, set off at five o'clock, for Mahogany Castle, the residence of the late Lord Mahogany, and which was now become the inheritance of the right honorable Lord Charles Oakley.

---

[82] Frederica Charlotte of Prussia (1767-1820). She became the Duchess of York and Albany when she married the Duke of York in 1791. The Duchess was known for her remarkably small feet, measuring 5.75 inches long and 1.75 across the instep. A drawing was made of her foot and published in 1791. F. W. Fairholt, *Costume in England: A History of Dress from the Earliest Period Until the Close of the Eighteenth Century* (London, 1860), 395.

VI

Captivating Scenery

Mahogany Castle was an ancient gothic building of the most imposing and venerable appearance, it had towers and battlements, and a moat: but never was there a spot more calculated for tender meditations than the extensive gardens which surrounded it.[83]

From the eminence on which the house was placed, as far as the eye could reach, it traced a silver meandering stream. In the distribution of the grounds, the hand of KNIGHT[84] had assisted, but not forced nature; each masterly stroke of his art had only served to bring to light beauties that lay concealed before, and too improve and cherish each gift the bounteous Goddess had lavished en this charming place.

A velvet lawn, gently sloped from the house down to the river, and served for pasture to some hundreds of sheep, which enriched the land, while they animated the scene. A rising wood stretched itself to a considerable distance on the east, its stems were washed by the river, and its feathered branches seemed to bend to receive the refreshing moisture. On the west, the eye wandered over an immense park; the ground was beautifully irregular; wild, and diversified with scattered herds of deer and cattle, groups of trees, with here and there a spire or a steeple peeping over their heads, and the view was terminated by rising hills.

The cold blasts of the North were kept off by some sheltering mountains; the sides were covered with the ilex, the laurel and the arbutus; and the summits were crowned with firs.

The shrubbery skirting the wood on the East, extended far to the South. It was adorned with a prodigious variety of flowering shrubs and curious plants,

---

[83] The source for this entire chapter was Hervey, *Melissa and Marcia*, II: 204-11.

[84] Hervey identified Capability Brown as the improver of the estate she described in *Melissa and Marcia*. Beckford substituted the name of Brown's adversary, Richard Payne Knight. The substitution of 'KNIGHT' in full capital letters could have been in recognition that the park Hervey described (essentially based upon scenes around the Beckford Fonthill Splendens estate) as 'beautifully irregular; wild and diversified' was more in accord with Knight's taste than Brown's. See R. J. Gemmett, *Beckford's Fonthill The Rise of a Romantic Icon* (Norwich: Michael Russell, 2003), 56-7.

collected from various parts of the world. A few temples, designed after the best ancient models, were judiciously placed, and a bridge, particularly light and elegant, thrown over the river.

But amongst the beauties of the scene, Lord Mahogany's cave was the most delightful spot.—In the spring, the approach to it seemed a terrestrial paradise. A gradual descent carried you from the house, through a winding path irregularly planted with firs and forest trees, skirted with laurels and flowering shrubs. Here and there the eye caught thorns in all the pride of blossom; their reign of beauty is but short, yet they stood alone on distinguished spots, and wreathed their trunks into many fantastic shapes.

The purple lilac in lovely clusters, and the unsullied white, vied with the Portugal laurel, and gelder rose, in beauty. Here festoons of libernum, and there the elegant acacia pleased the eye, while the air was perfumed with the united fragrance of sweet-briar and violets;

The musk-rose, and the well-attired wood-bine,
With cowslips wan that hang the pensive head.[85]

In wandering thus through a labyrinth of sweets, sometimes you caught a view of the adjacent country, and saw the water glitter through the trees; but often the closing branches confined the eye to the delightful spot around. As you advanced, the shrubs gave way entirely to forest trees—majestic oaks, elms, chesnuts, and beeches formed into a spacious grove. At first their tall straight stems appeared like columns set at convenient distances from each other; by degrees they pressed closer together; their bright tints disappeared; the deep recesses of the grove were darkened with the solemn gloom of cedars, and mournful cypresses, now quite impervious to the rays of the sun. The paths became more numerous and intricate, till they brought you to some irregular steps cut in a rock; the light insensibly stole upon you as you descended; and at the foot of the steps you found the entrance of a spacious cave. All here was hushed and silent, save that the trickling drops of a purling rill struck your ear, while it softly bent its way toward the parent stream. A broken arch opened to your view the broad clear expanse of the lake, covered with numerous aquatic fowl, and weeping willows adorning its banks.

Round this cave no gaudy flowers were ever permitted to bloom; this spot was sacred to pale lilies and violets. An outlet, at first scarcely perceived in the cave, carried you through a winding passage to an immense amphitheatre,

[85] John Milton, *Lycidas*, ll. 146-7.

formed by a multitude of irregular rocks; some bold and abrupt, others covered with ivy, perriwinkles, and wall-flowers. One of these grottos was destined for a bath, and ornamented with branches of coral, brilliant spars, and curious shells. A lucid spring filled a marble bason in the centre, and then losing itself for a moment under ground, came dashing and sparkling forth at the extremity of the cave, and took its course over some shining pebbles to the lake below. Here stretched supinely on a bed of moss, the late Lord Mahogany would frequently pass the sultry hours of the day, and here its present worthy possessor Lord Charles Oakley would sometimes also indulge himself. The grove, though less charming than when enlivened by the sweet song of the nightingale, and adorned with the tender foliage of the spring, was still delightful. His Lordship, to compensate for the loss of the lily and the violet, had substituted the tuberose, jessamine, and orange trees. The pots were concealed in the earth, and they appeared natives of the cave. Here all his thoughts were engrossed by the object of his flame. Here he formed schemes of delusive joys, stifled the rising sigh, stopped the flowing tear, and in social converse with his dear friend Henry Lambert would oftentimes smoke a comfortable pipe, when the soft radiance of the moon played upon the pearly bosom of the adjacent waters.

VII

Severe Treatment

Don Pedro having returned to Spain on very important business, the wretchedly forlorn Amelia knew not how to fill up the miserable interval that must necessarily pass before his return, when one day, having taken it into her head to go a trout fishing, at the corner of a copse of hazle and brush wood, she was suddenly surrounded by six men with black crape over their faces, who, having gagged her, bore her to a distant mansion, which she did not at first recognise, but which she soon discovered to be the abode of the Marchioness of Oakley. Having entered, they crossed a prodigious large hall, which in days of yore, had often feasted hundreds of vassals and dependents of the Oakley family, but its neglected walls shewed it had long been deserted.— A solemn stillness reigned through the building, no noise was heard but the echoing sound of their footsteps on the pavement, and the distant crowing of that domestic male bird, which with piercing note cried Cock-a-doodle-do.[86]

Having passed through many windings and passages, and ascended a vast staircase covered with old family pictures, and after traversing a *suite* of rooms, some without windows, others unfurnished, at length they arrived at an apartment wainscoted with oak, with old-fashioned chairs, covered with dark blue velvet, and which received its light from grated casements, nearly as far from the floor as from the ceiling.

Within, was a bedchamber in the same style, with an enormous sized bed, the tester of which was fastened to the ceiling, and the walls hung with old-fashioned tapestry.

One of the men, shewed her a small servant's chamber, and taking the gag out of her delicate mouth informed her that these were her apartments. They then all joined in a loud chorus of 'Rule Brittania,' and departed.

Amelia who had trembled from head to foot ever since she had entered this odious house, and had a *presentment* of her fate, cast a mournful look around, and burst into a violent agony of tears.

---

[86] The source for this passage to the end of the chapter was Hervey, I: 238-44. Greibel, 401-2.

Dinner was soon after served by an old woman, whom Amelia could not get to speak a word, for in fact, she was both deaf and dumb, besides the having a nasty whitlow on her middle finger which had tormented her above a fortnight. The repast consisted of a dish of sprats, a bason of boiled tripe, a dozen roasted larks, some broiled kidnies, a suet pudding, and a roast duck.

In the evening the Marchioness made her appearance, with a stern countenance, and said she had some business to settle, but that she should see her again before her departure. 'Your departure,' cried the terrified Amelia, 'can you think of leaving me here? You had better kill me at once.' The Marchioness made no answer, but immediately left the room.

She returned, however, to supper; no conversation passed, and as soon as it was over, retired, and sent Mrs. Dorothy Webster to Amelia, whose spirits were so totally subdued, that she suffered herself, without speaking, to be put to bed.

The next morning the Marchioness came to take her leave, when Amelia, with a torrent of tears, flung herself upon her knees, and in the humblest accents sued for mercy. Lady Oakley raised her up, and placing her on a chair, 'Compose yourself, Madam,' said she, 'and submit patiently to your fate; here I am determined you shall remain; and your behavior will decide, whether your imprisonment shall be temporary, or only terminate with your life. Your reasonable commands Mrs. Dorothy Webster will obey, your wants shall be supplied, but nothing more.'

She then hastily rushed out of the room, and after sending Mrs. Dorothy Webster to Amelia, immediately quitted the house.

Nothing could be more deplorable than Amelia's condition, she raved, screamed, tore her hair, and refused all consolation. Alone in this dismal prison, never seeing any creature but Mrs. Dorothy Webster; from frantic fits of despair, she fell into a stupid melancholy, would frequently whistle 'Britons strike home'[87] for the hour together, talked about the Rights of Man like a maniac,[88] and drank lemonade like a fish.

---

[87] The title of a song from the opera *Bonduca* (1695) by Henry Purcell (1658?-1695).

[88] i.e. Thomas Paine's *Rights of Man* (1791-2), a staunch supporter of the French and American revolutions and vocal critic of the oppressive tactics of the British government.

VIII

A Water Party

After some days passed in a disagreeable confinement, Amelia turned her thoughts on speculative philosophy, and soon discovered the power of the human Will, by a proper exertion of which, she could conquer the approach of sleep and hunger with a marvellous facility.

The Marchioness in consequence of these favourable symptoms in her fair prisoner's mind, invited a large party to go upon the lake, in a very magnificent barge, which had formerly belonged to the stationer's company,[89] and which had been knocked down to her ladyship at a private auction, for fourteen pounds twelve shillings and ninepence halfpenny.

The company was very brilliant, and the weather prodigiously fine; they were all dressed in their richest cloathes, and looked as elegant as carrots when newly scraped by the industrious care of a handsome cookmaid. The wind was South-West, and the little fishes sported in the vessel's silver *wake* with a fascinating gaiety; then unfortunately Lucinda Howard, stretching forward to catch a cormorant, slipped overboard, and in a moment disappeared. General Barton immediately burst into tears, the Marchioness fainted, and Amelia fell into strong hystericks. At this interesting moment the Rev. Mr. Squares,[90] so renowned for his valuable criticisms, for his love of royalty, and detestation of liberty, jumped upon the deck, and jerking away his spectacles with uncommon grace, exclaimed 'Good lack a day,' then curling up his nose with a cynical twist peculiar to himself, plunged beneath the waves, and seized the drowning Lucinda by the locks,

---

[89] The Stationers' company maintained an elegant barge which was used on Lord Mayor's day to accompany the Lord Mayor in an elaborate aquatic procession to Lambeth Palace to present the Archbishop of Canterbury with copies of their almanacs they published every year. Edward Walford, *Old and New London. The Southern Suburbs* (London, 1878), 6: 442.

[90] This is Revd Robert Nares (1753-1829), philologist and editor. He established the *British Critic* in 1793, a target of Beckford's satire for its Tory political bias. Beckford used Nares's name in a variant text of *Modern Novel Writing* before substituting the name Squares. See section on 'Textual Notes' for Beckford's additional emendations. Cyrus Redding, Beckford's first biographer, also identified Squares as 'Archdeacon Nares,' describing him as a 'violent Tory' in *Memoirs of William Beckford of Fonthill* (London, 1859), II: 188; 212.

Like a rich triumph in one hand he bore her,
And with the other dash'd the saucy waves,
That throng'd and press'd to rob him of his prize.[91]

Mr. Bilbo, a learned coadjutor of the Divine,[92] was for some time so shocked and overcome, that he could not speak. At length, pointing his left foot towards the dangerous element, he cried out in original Greek Βραυω;[93] then seizing a heavy translation of Herodotus in a fit of distraction he hurled it furiously at the celebrated Mr. Gifford's head, which being of a very solid texture, received no kind of injury. The blow, however, awakened the spleen of the satirist, who immediately expressed his sensations by the two following excellent and extemporaneous verses.

By Jove I will lampoon you all,
Except Sam Slybore—great and small.[94]

Now Sam Slybore was laughing in his sleeve during the whole transaction, and declared he would in the course of twenty-four hours produce a painting of the whole scene with his accustomed *sincerity*. This alarmed the Marchioness and the rest of the ladies, when Amelia archly demanded of the Limner 'were

---

[91] From Thomas Otway (1652-1685), *Venice Preserv'd* (1682), Act I, i. The actual lines read:

Like a rich conquest in one hand I bore her,
And with the other dashed the saucy waves,
That throng'd and pressed to rob me of my prize:

[92] This is Revd William Beloe (1756-1817), divine and co-editor of the *British Critic*. He was a translator of the classics, including *The History of Herodotus*, which he published in 1791. Beckford used Beloe's name in a variant text of *Modern Novel Writing* before substituting the name Bilbo. See section on 'Textual Notes' for Beckford's additional emendations. Redding also confirmed this identification. Redding, II: 188.

[93] Beckford uses Greek letters here to create the word 'Bravo.'

[94] Sam Slybore is John Hoppner (1758-1810), portrait painter and close friend of Gifford. Gifford dedicated the *Mæviad* to Hoppner and commemorated their friendship in the lines that began:

Thou too, MY HOPPNER! if my wish availed,
Should'st praise the strain that but for thee had failed:
Thou knowest, when Indolence possessed me all,
How oft I roused at thy inspiring call;
Burst from the Syren's fascinating power,
And gave the Muse thou lovest, one studious hour.
Proud of thy friendship, while the voice of fame
Pursues thy merits with a loud acclaim ... (ll. 339-46)

In a variant text of *Modern Novel Writing*, Beckford wrote '*my* Hopner' before substituting Sam Slybore, thereby alluding to these lines from the poem. See section on 'Textual Notes' for Beckford's additional emendations.

not you educated at Buckingham House?'[95] Every body took the joke, and in
a few moments they all landed with the utmost harmony and good humour.

During this period of time, the Reverend Mr. Squares who had dragged
Lucinda to the shore, was endeavouring to recover her by putting in practice
all the means which have been directed by the Humane Society,[96] and at
length he happily succeeded—It was then that the meek Lucinda gazing on
the Parson with ineffable rapture, exclaimed, 'now the secret is discovered, the
cat is let out of the bag, you my charming Squares, you are the man I love and
have long loved—I have languished many months, but now I look to you for
comfort, you have saved my life, you know my mind, O Squares!'

The divine, though very much flattered to find that Lucinda Howard was
so deeply smitten, yet being terribly drenched by the water, stood mournfully
drooping, and had a similar appearance to a rat half-drowned. His natural
asperity however soon returned, and he declared that he would be—if he
did not cut them all up in his next Review,[97] which determination the great
Gifford highly approved of, and Sam Slybore

Grinn'd horribly a ghastly smile, to find
His friends would be abused.[98]

Bilbo said nothing, but he paid it off with thinking—and Amelia wittily observed
to him—'The still sow sucks the most draught.' Lucinda, having thanked Mr.
Squares, the Marchioness, Sam Slybore, and the rest of the company, for their
kind solicitude, retired—being determined to prepare a copy of verses fit for
the eye of the immortal Squares. She therefore took a dose of salts, and after
seven or eight *movements*, produced the following panegyrical ode, which she
presented to her beloved Squares the next morning at breakfast, and which was
highly applauded by all the company, but especially by Mr. Gifford and the
Painter.

---

[95] The 'joke' derives from a commonly held view at this time that Hoppner was an illegitimate offspring
of George III and educated under the king's direction at Buckingham House. The rumour persisted partly
because the artist never discouraged it. William McKay and W. Roberts, *John Hoppner, R. A.* (London,
1914), xv. Ironically, Hoppner did a portrait of Beckford ca. 1800.

[96] The Royal Humane Society, founded in 1774. They gave awards to those individuals who were
successful at resuscitating drowning victims.

[97] A variant text identifies this review as the 'British Critic.' See section on 'Textual Notes' for Beckford's
additional emendations.

[98] Milton, *Paradise Lost*, Bk. II, l. 846.

Ode to my Dear Squares[99]

O thou, my Squares! best formed to show,
The right and wrong of things below,
    To thee I dedicate the song—
Prime Parson of this happy land,
The foremost of the critic band,
    The terror of the scribbling throng!

Whether in pride of mental might,
Thou wagest literary fight,
    With spectacles upon thy nose,
Or quaffing gay Sam Slybore's glass,
Thou toastest many a buxom lass,
    Alike for thee my bosom glows.

---

[99] This poem was addressed originally to Revd Nares who 'wagest literary fight/ With spectacles upon thy nose.' In a variant text Beckford used the title 'Ode to my Nostrils' and incorporated the following footnote to the poem: 'Lucinda, to avoid the imputation of pedantry, adopted the English word Nostrils instead of the Latin *Nares*, and it certainly has a more poetical effect.' Beckford, according to Redding, often called Nares 'Nastilo,' referring to the prominence of his nose. Redding, II, 212. Hoppner's portrait of Nares also emphasized the spectacles he habitually wore. See section on 'Textual Notes' for Beckford's additional emendations. The following is the variant text of the poem:

Ode to my Nostrils

O thou, my Nostrils! formed to show,
The right and wrong of things below,
    To thee I dedicate the song—
Prime Parson of this happy land,
The foremost of the critic band,
    The terror of the scribbling throng!

Whether in pride of mental might,
Thou wagest literary fight,
    With spectacles upon thy nose,
Or quaffing gay *my* Hopner's glass,
Thou toastest many a buxom lass,
    Alike for thee my bosom glows.

Whether thou teachest readers vile,
When they should frown, and when should smile,
    By thy scholastic rigid rules;
Or in a haughty cleric passion
Mendest the judgment of the nation,
    Proving it but a nest of fools;

Still will I love thee, Nostril's dear!
Still will I heave the sigh sincere,
    Thou hast preserved Lucinda's life!
And as thou plunged'st in the water,
To save an honest Person's daughter,
    Make her an honest Parson's wife!

And I, my love! will join with thee,
Against the cause of liberty,
    And all its daring friends to scold,
Tyrants and sycophants we'll praise,
To pensioners our voices raise,
    And touch like them the BRITISH GOLD.

Then Gifford with his lumbring line,
Shall swear our efforts are divine,
    Beloe shall gaze with look demure;
My Hopner kindest, best of men!
Shall add his pencil to the pen,
    And paint us all in car'cature.

Whether thou teachest readers vile,
When they should frown, and when should smile,
   By thy scholastic rigid rules;
Or in a haughty cleric passion
Mendest the judgment of the nation,
   Proving it but a nest of fools;

Still will I love thee, Squares so dear!
Still will I heave the sigh sincere,
   Thou hast preserved Lucinda's life!
And as thou plunged'st in the water,
To save an honest Person's daughter,
   Make her an honest Parson's wife!

And I, my love! will join with thee,
Against the cause of liberty,
   And all its daring friends to scold,
Tyrants and sycophants we'll praise,
To pensioners our voices raise,
   And touch like them the BRITISH GOLD.

Then Gifford, with his lumbring line,
Shall swear our efforts are divine,
   Bilbo shall gaze with look demure;
Sam Slybore kindest, best of men!
Shall add his pencil to the pen,
   And paint us all in car'cature.

IX

A Remarkable Occurrence

Lucinda's unfortunate passion every day acquired more strength, till at length she rapidly declined in health, while the dear object of her choice treated her with the most unpardonable neglect. Occupied in his literary pursuits, and in his grand endeavour to correct the public taste, he had no time to throw away in sighs and tenderness. Mr. Gifford, on the contrary, was particularly attentive to her, and would frequently gaze upon her with ineffable sensibility. Nay, such was the increasing violence of his regard, that he actually presented her with his divine satirical poem called the Mæviad,[100] which he had been delivered of with dreadful pains, and which had cost him infinite labour.— As, however, it had no sale, he thought he might spare her one copy, because it could not injure his interest, and might be considered as a token of his regard.

This exquisite goodness on the part of Mr. Gifford made a deep impression on the heart of the charming Lucinda, but in vain, her affections were already fixed on a faithless, 'gallant, gay Lothario,'[101] and all the rest of mankind were of no consequence to her.

She pined in thought.[102]

She did indeed, and in a few weeks grew so extremely 'green and yellow,' that it was disagreeable to look upon her. Had Mr. Squares felt for her those gentle sensations which correspond with her internal emotions, no doubt they might have been happy in the extreme: but alas! in this transitory world, the fairest hopes are too frequently blighted, and the best pretensions not seldom obumbrated by despair. Lucinda Howard was beautifully pathetic,

---

[100] The *Mæviad* was Gifford's satire against the poor state of contemporary drama.

[101] Nicholas Rowe, *The Fair Penitent*, V, i, l. 37.

[102] Shakespeare, *Twelfth Night*, II, iv, l. 115.

and possessed a mind of the finest texture, therefore the coldness of her beloved Clergyman affected her too deeply, and in her exquisite agitations she wandered through the wilds of fancy with marvellous pertinacity. Not but she had hopes of softening his obdurate nature by time and opportunity, yet the difficulty was great, and in the interim she was liable to all those little incidental inconveniencies which arise from ill requited affection, and the workings of a generous, but a too tender, heart. She therefore seized the first occasion that offered to send him the following composition.

Ode to the Moon

Meek Queen of Night! who gliding o'er the glade,
Art so averse from shade,
All hail!
Whether upon the flow'ry vale
Or on the Woodland height,
Thou shed'st thy stream of silver light;—
I still admire thee, very much,
Or when thou deign'st to touch
The rocks magnificent that o'er the sea
Rise in sublime deformity;—
For thou art wondrous fair; and thy full Orb
Can all mankind entrance, and this rich globe absorb.

Thy soft Eye glistering on the vernal grove,
Awakes its feather'd Choiresters to love,
Or when the nightingale begins to pause,
And the lone Shepherd's mild attention draws,
Thou addest to th' enchanting scene,
By telling thy pale beams to intervene—
Thus when my Critic Clergyman appears,
I melt in anguish, and in tears,
Because he is indifferent and cold,
Nor am I very young, nor is he very old.

Strike the loud drum, and wake the merry flute,
With dub a-dub-a-dub, and toot, toot, toot,
Let the shrill trumpet Tarra-tarra cry,
And the sweet viol breathe its melody.
While to the glancing moon my song I pour,

> And tell of him I ever must adore;
> Whose winning smiles, whose voice, whose gait to me
> Are one eternal source of joy and extasy.

When the wondering Mr. Squares had read this delightful effusion, he called for a glass of gin and water, and with more than his usual good nature, exclaimed, 'Thus endeth the second lesson!' [103]

---

[103] A reference to the New Testament from the order of how the Holy Scripture is to be read in *The Book of Common Prayer*. The Old Testament is appointed for the first lesson at morning and evening prayer; the New Testament as the second lesson.

X

A Digression and a Dream

During the progress of this little work, the greatest care has been taken to avoid confusion, and to establish throughout, a general consistency of character, and a regular succession of events. To this praise the publication must have some claim, whatever defects may be found in the style, the sentiments, or the poetry. But to return.

Henry Lambert having obtained the rank of Colonel became an object of much interest to the first societies in London, where a number of elegant young Ladies, who have perhaps more beauty than fortune, are always to be disposed of to Gentlemen of honor and consideration. He however, was totally absorbed in the contemplation of the happiness he might have shared with the incomparable and lovely Arabella, if such a succession of untoward circumstances had not prevented him. As his affection for the glorious constitution of his country was unbounded, and as he had at all times a proper contempt for the hunger and sufferings of the poor, so in an equal degree he respected the ornamental part of society, consisting of Lords, Aldermen, Parliament Men, Crimps,[104] Justices of the Peace, Bishops, Deans, Arch-deacons, and Attorneys.

One evening Henry finding himself indisposed, retired early to his bed, and presently fell asleep. The dream he had this night made such an impression upon him, that the very moment day-light appeared, he wrote it down as follows, for the entertainment and instruction of his friends.

The Dream

Methought I was thrown upon an island in the Atlantic ocean which was crowded with inhabitants, and the ports of which were full of vessels from all parts of the world. Its surface was covered with abundance, and every countenance I saw denoted chearfulness, prosperity, and content: But after

---

[104] A person who serves in an unsavoury activity on behalf of another—literally a pimp.

a little time I beheld a band of ruffians possess themselves of all the power of government, and divide amongst themselves the riches of the land. The liberties of the people were speedily annihilated, they were plunged into destructive wars to gratify the selfishness and ambition of their rulers, they were reduced to famine by every species of the basest monopoly, and the honest and industrious poor were consigned to ignominy and treated with contempt. Then the people assembled in great multitudes to complain, and petitioned their oppressors to grant them some relief, but they found none, their just remonstrances were deemed seditious and treasonable, and the men who had thus seized the reins of authority, published an order forbidding all persons to assemble, or even to murmur; and afterwards a decree was passed that all the tongues of all the complainants should be cut out as a proper punishment for their audacity. When this *strong measure* was carried into execution, there was a dead silence throughout the nation, and order and tranquility were pretty generally restored. Now methought the name of this strange country was, THE ISLAND OF MUM.[105]

---

[105] Lambert's dream becomes a vehicle for Beckford's strongest attack against the Pitt administration for passing the exceedingly repressive Treasonable and Seditious Practices Act and the Seditious Assemblies Act on 18 December 1795.

XI

Female Frailty, and a Misfortune

As the elegant Lucinda was one morning walking upon the terrace of Lady Fairville's garden, ruminating upon her sad and hopeless destiny, she observed a youth sleeping on a bank of daiseys, fashionably attired. She started at the sight and faintly screamed, while he, at the sound of her angelic voice sprang towards her, and folding his fond arms around her, professed himself the eternal slave of her beauty and attraction. 'O!' exclaimed he with the most wild and energetic passion, 'O thou mirror of superhuman excellence, thou soft sustainer of all earthly good, to every zone I will declare the ardor of that flame which now consumes my heart, thou art a divinity of the first order, a lambent fire of exquisite delight that plays upon the wings of fancy, and settles both the judgment and the wish! How beautifully fall those luxuriant tresses in soft profusion on a neck of snow, which seems as if it were just tinged by the last weak blush of evening. Ha! those lips, how inconceivably tempting, those eyes how penetrating, how brilliant, how expressive—chin, nose, mouth, teeth, arms, elbows, breast and shape, how beyond all conception captivating and enchanting!' She now reclined her head upon his burning bosom, while many a dewy drop moistened her glowing cheek. Her sensibility yielded to the impression of so much tenderness and truth, she clasped him tenderly in a soft embrace and almost fainted.

There happened to be a hermitage at no great distance from the scene of action—it was made of moss, and in it was a couch for Lady Fairville to repose herself, after the fatigues of company and cards. Thither the gallant handsome youth bore the yielding Lucinda 'nothing loth,' and there, if we may use the words of Shakespeare, he

Robbed her of that which naught enriched him,
And made her poor indeed.[106]

---

[106] *Othello*, III, iii, ll. 159-61. Iago expressing concern about his good name and reputation:

But he that filches from me my good name
Robs me of that which not enriches him,
And makes me poor indeed.

The two lovers passed several hours in this heavenly retreat, vowing eternal fidelity to each other,

And mingling soft discourse with kisses sweet.

As at length, however, it became necessary for them to put a period to so interesting a tete-a-tete, Lucinda, with her accustomed prudence, reminded him that it was time to depart, and he instantly obeyed her command, but not till she had given him one balmy parting salute, and had promised to marry him the first opportunity. To which, the enamoured youth being overcome by the fineness of his sensations, could make no reply.

As Lucinda was tripping across the lawn towards the house, she unfortunately met Mr. Squares and Mr. Gifford, who were taking an *abusive* walk,

As is their custom in an afternoon.

She was shocked at the sight of these two cynics, and though she was somewhat relieved to find that Sam Slybore was not with them, yet the severity of their aspect had such an effect upon her delicate nerves, that she immediately fell sick with a bilious fever, and notwithstanding all the care of the Satirist, and the pious prayers of the Parson, before twelve o'clock on the next day, she was as dead as Julius Caesar. The following beautiful epitaph upon her was written by a learned and ingenious schoolmaster of Dedham in Essex; it was composed in less than eight months, and is engraved upon her tombstone in Banbury church-yard.

The Epitaph

Here lies the body of Lucinda Howard,
Who neither ugly was, nor false, nor froward;
But good and pretty, as this verse declares,
And sav'd from drowning by his Reverence Squares.
But small the 'vantage, for she scarce was *dried*,
Before she made a sad faux pas—and DIED.

XII

A Wide Spreading Calamity

The sudden death of the unfortunate Lucinda Howard, having thrown a great damp over the company, it was thought adviseable to adjourn to the mansion of Don Pedro de Gonzales, who having been appointed Ambassador from Spain, led his charming Amelia through every round of animating pleasures which his situation enabled him to pursue.

As his attachment to the heaven-born Mr. Pitt was great, and as he honoured the transparent virtues of the wise Lord Grenville and the humane Mr. Windham,[107] so he passed his time in the most splendid luxury amongst the principal placemen,[108] pensioners, and other worthies of the court. There is however no accounting for accidents as we all know by fatal experience, for on the third day after the arrival of the party, owing to a copper stew-pan in which some celery had been cooked, every person present was seized with convulsions about eleven o'clock at night, and the following Ladies and Gentlemen departed this life in the course of twenty four hours: Amelia de Gonzales, General Barton, Lady Langley, Major Pemberton, the Marchioness of Oakley, Lord Charles Oakley, Doctor Philberd, Miss Warley, the two Miss Pebleys, Miss Maleverer, and Sir Sidney Walker. This terrible catastrophe occasioned much bustle throughout the county, and various opinions were formed upon the subject; however, as the coroner's inquest brought them all in lunatics, so the affair went off with more spirit and decorum than could at first have been imagined. Fortunately none of the great political personages were present at this fatal dinner, otherwise the country at large would have suffered an irreparable loss.

---

[107] William Wyndham, Lord Grenville (1759-1834) served as Foreign Secretary under Pitt and was a supporter of repressive domestic legislation to maintain order in Britain. William Windham (1750-1810) became known for his consistently strong resistance to any peace negotiations with France.

[108] A person appointed to a government position as a reward for political support without regard for meeting the qualifications for holding such a position.

XIII

A Philosopher

When Arabella heard of the dreadful misfortune that had befallen her friends, she resigned herself to the most excruciating sorrow, and frequently reflected with all the poignancy of despair, on the conduct of her beloved Henry. To Colonel and Lady Maria Lambert she therefore determined to apply for that consolation which her immediate agonies demanded.

Having dressed herself in a blue robe with a yellow sash, she departed with the faithful Margaret Grimes, in quest of him who could alone administer relief to her perturbed soul.

It was now autumn, and the harvest was every where got in, when tempted by the beauty of a rich country, the two fair travellers descended one evening from their chaise, to repose themselves upon the bank of a rivulet that ran murmuring with a shallow stream among groves, and lawns, and flowers. While they were here enjoying the rural solitude of the scene, and imbibing the wholesome freshness of the air, they were surprized by the appearance of a man very much worn with years, leaning upon a staff, who advanced slowly towards them.[109] His beard was long, full, and white as the mountain snow, his eyes were sunk deep in his head, his countenance was melancholy, and with a faultering voice he thus addressed them.

'Ladies, it is now above sixty years since I retired from the world into yonder neighbouring wood, where I have built a hut which defends me from the inclemencies of the season. My food consists of the simplest herbs, and I slake my thirst at the lucid spring. I was turned of thirty years when I quitted the unmeaning bustle of the world, to dedicate my life to solitude and reflection. I had found, alas! that my friends were false, and the woman of my heart was faithless; I therefore shunned the society of mankind; for to live in a croud without confidence or attachment, is a misery insupportable. Here I have employed myself in useful study, and occupied my mind with deep researches,

---

[109] Arabella's meeting with the philosopher hermit begins Beckford's parody of Fielding's Man of the Hill story in *Tom Jones*. Source first identified by Archibald B. Shepperson, *The Novel in Motley A History of the Burlesque Novel in English* (New York: Octagon Books, 1967), 105.

which, though they shall never benefit the human race, have served to enlarge my soul, and to render it more capable of future happiness. I have calculated the succession of seconds passed since the creation of the world, I have discovered the average number of hairs that grow upon the heads of all mankind, I have found out with great trouble how many half pints of water are contained in this terraqueous globe; the leaves in yonder forest have all been counted by me, and I hope in a little time to be exactly informed, how many millions of words womankind utter every twenty-four hours throughout all the world. This, with afterwards reducing the words into letters, will be the occupation of the ensuing year, and you must allow that it will be time nobly and meritoriously employed. I find that at four o'clock this morning, I had lived precisely 2,932,949,000 seconds, yet how soon are they fled! a portion of life containing 33945 days is granted unto few, but how short is even such a period! nor do my tears ever cease to flow, when I reflect upon the destruction of animal life, made by the human inhabitants of this earth. More rapacious than the mountain wolf, more savage than the tyger of the desert, each individual gorges himself with blood. I can prove that the most delicate female by the time she attains the age of twenty five, never fails to have eaten to her own share a flock of sheep consisting of 167, beeves 39, calves 48, hogs, 51, chickens 3256, besides 1840 ducks, with turkeys, pigeons, partridges, pheasants, hares, and wildfowl, in proportion—add to these as many fishes as would satisfy the largest whale for a twelve month, together with an abundance of corn, wine, oil, herbs, fruit, and other necessaries.' At these words Arabella and Margaret Grimes burst into an immoderate fit of laughing, which so much affected the old man that he walked off in disdain. The two travellers now began to make some shrewd remarks upon the different occupations of men, and the various causes of their pursuits and studies, when Arabella instantly called to mind the excellence of her Henry, and seizing Margaret Grimes by the hair with great energy, vowed eternal fidelity to him.

On the following day they pursued their journey in the waggon, and arrived at length in perfect safety at their lodgings in Conduit Street, which had been previously taken for a Bishop's daughter, by an Alderman. The promised pleasures of the grand metropolis delighted the tender heart of Arabella, and the hopes of again seeing her dear Henry, conveyed the strongest sensations of rapture to her breast, while Margaret, the faithful Margaret, formed schemes of conquest, to which, through life she had hitherto been a stranger.

XIV

A Visit to a Minister of State

Since the fatal rencontre with Arabella that had so disturbed the peace of Henry, he had left off many of those idle amusements which add but little to the general stock of harmless pleasure, and too frequently mislead the mind into a labyrinth of woe.

He therefore called upon Dr. Sanderson at his elegant villa, to ask his advice relative to his own future conduct with Arabella; besides, he wished to be informed whether the worthy Doctor had really adopted those democratic principles which he had been reported to have done, for Henry was very unwilling to withdraw his friendship and regard from any man without very sufficient reason. Lawyer Blackingson had indeed circulated many cruel reports to the injury of the poor Doctor's reputation, but the general opinion of Blackingson was so unfavourable, that Henry thought it beneath him to pay much attention to his malignant stories, knowing that the fellow, though himself a bit of a Farmer, had no greater delight upon earth than to oppress the poor to the utmost of his power, and to beat his maids when occasion offered.

In this emergency therefore Henry cropped his hair according to the prevailing mode, and pulling on his boots and spurs waited on Mr. Pitt to thank him for the care he had so kindly taken of the British nation. As Henry, by the death of the Marchioness of Oakley, was become a man of immense property, with two Boroughs at his command, so the heaven-born minister received him with more than his common candour, and presented him with a goblet of sherry and two macaroons. Henry, overcome by such a testimony of regard, and captivated by the condescension of so great a man, politely offered him in return a pinch of snuff, and with pleasing diffidence demanded if THE ACT FOR GENERAL SILENCE was passed. The great Rose[110] assured him it was,

---

[110] George Rose (1744-1818), Secretary Treasury and staunch supporter of Pitt's policies. The scarcity of bread due to weak harvests and the heavy burden of taxes to support the war that the general population had to bear were causing widespread upheaval at this time. When George III opened Parliament in October 1795, he was greeted with shouts of 'Give us bread!' 'No war!' and 'Down with Pitt.' When peace efforts failed in May 1796, Pitt again responded by increasing taxes causing riots to occur in response. Cestre, 121.

and that Lord Grenville, Lord Mansfield, Mr. Windham and himself were the happiest of men, in spite of the high price of bread, and the encreasing weight of taxes, which he jocularly observed did not affect them. Henry getting more intimate, and more easy in the presence of such sublime personages, earnestly entreated to have a bason of pea soup, but this Pitt absolutely refused, because he was under the necessity of going to the house.[III]

Here then the conference ended for the present, and Henry returned home in the highest spirits, and being in a finely animated mood, immediately wrote a comedy which he carried the next morning to the manager of Covent Garden theatre, who received it favourably, and as it had no plot, and was full of tumbling, kicking, breaking, and buffonery, so it met with universal applause, and gained the approbation of Mr. Astley the elder,[112] who has long presided over the amusements of the Public with wonderful eclat; and who enjoys the holy patronage of his Royal Highness the Bishop of Osnabourg, Duke of York.[113]

Arabella in the mean time indulged her delicate fancy in all the softness of romantic love, and when the moon scattered her pale yellow tints on the sycamore grove, she wandered forth to all appearance a

Pensive Nun devout and pure,
Sober, steadfast and demure.[114]

Seated upon a favourite green bench on the margin of a bubbling stream, she would remain for hours reading her beloved Ariosto[115] and eating golden pippins, while the tears would incessantly 'chase one another down her

---

[III] i. e. House of Commons

[112] Philip Astley (1742-1814), equestrian performer, considered to be the father of the modern circus. He created the first circus ring or amphitheatre in London in 1770. Although destroyed by fire, it became The Royal Amphitheatre of Arts under the patronage of the Prince of Wales and the Duke of York in 1794. His events, which attracted large crowds, were known for trick riding on horseback, staged battle scenes, and gradually expanded to include other kinds of performers, such as clowns, acrobats, rope dancers and aerialists. *Encyclopædia Britannica* (2002), I: 651-2.

[113] Frederick Augustus, Duke of York and Albany (1763-1827), second son of George III, was elected to the bishopric of Osnaburg in 1764.

[114] Milton, *Il Penseroso*, ll. 31-2.

[115] Ludovico Ariosto (1474-1533), Italian poet and author of the epic romance, *Orlando Furioso*, one of Beckford's favourite works as a young man.

innocent nose,' [116] as she reflected on the capricious instability of her heart's dear lord, her handsome gallant Henry Lambert. To divert her melancholy she at times would yield her soul to the delusions of poetry. And one evening being in rather better spirits than usual, produced the following enigma, which those persons who can discover its meaning will find to be a *chef d'oeuvre* of the art.

Enigma

I'm as firm as a rock, and as weak as a reed,
As slow as a snail, and as swift as a steed,
As fat as a porpoise, yet thin as a rake,
As pliant as ozier, though stiff as a stake.
I'm a giant, a dwarf, a lion, a hare,
And by fetters constrain'd, am as free as the air.
Extremely deform'd, yet a beauty complete,
Very tall, very short, and tho' dirty am neat.
I can fly like an eagle, but can't leave the ground,
Am exactly a square, yet am perfectly round;
I'm as heavy as lead, and as light as a fly;
And am at a distance whenever I'm nigh.
Tho' I talk all day long, I'm as mute as a fish;
And tho' wanting all things have nothing to wish.
I'm as red as a rose, yet as black as a crow;
Am the friend of mankind, yet am every man's foe.
I'm a king and a beggar, a drab and a queen,
And while charming *all eyes*, am not fit to be seen.

---

[116] Shakespeare, *As You Like It*, II, i, ll. 38-40:

        and the big round tears
      Cours'd one another down his innocent nose
      In piteous chase;

XV

A Pleasant Evening

There is but little resource in the human heart in times of emergency, unless nature adds a redundancy of imagination to regulate the impetuosity that springs from discordant sentiments. Of this the dear fascinating Arabella was more convinced than ever, and therefore determined to open her little cottage for the reception of a small party, whose conversation and remarks might tend to withdraw her agitated mind from the contemplation of her adorable Henry.

The card table was accordingly *set*, and Mr. Bilbo, having cut in as partner with the beautiful Miss Bradwell, for a rubber at whist, was asked by that Lady if he had written his Arabian story books himself.[117] The pride of the author revolted at the question, and he begged leave to observe, that however he might like to cut up the works of other persons, he was nevertheless as *sore* as any body when his own were attacked. As the growling Gifford saw that matters began to wear a serious aspect, he wished to enliven the company by reading a few extracts from his ode to the Reverend Mr. Ireland, written in imitation of Horace.[118] Taking therefore a pinch of black-guard from Mr. Squares's box, and nodding gracefully to Sam Slybore, he began as follows.

---

[117] William Beloe published some Arabic stories in the third volume of *Miscellanies, Consisting of Classical Extracts, and Oriental Apologues* (London, 1795). Beckford may be alluding to the fact that these stories were not translated by Beloe but by Patrick Russell (1727-1805), author of *The Natural History of Aleppo* (1794). See ALF LAYLA wa LALA [*The Book of a thousand nights and a night*], Brill's Encyclopedia of Islam (Leiden, 1999).

[118] This ode appears as a footnote to the *Mæviad*, published in 1795. Revd John Ireland (1761-1842), vicar of Croydon, Surrey, a close friend of Gifford and author of *Five discourses, containing certain arguments for and against the reception of Christianity by the antient Jews and Greeks* (1796). Beckford's transcribes extracts from the poem almost word for word, and then creates an elaborate set of footnotes for it to mock Gifford's habit of adding extensive self-serving notes to his own texts to draw the reader's attention to the intrinsic beauties of the text. As Cyrus Redding noted: 'The self-conceit of Gifford before he became the wielder of the Quarterly tomahawk [*Quarterly Review*], and the dread writers not of the party he supported, was a constant theme of periodical publications in that day,—not, indeed, for his attachment to the betting-stand, but as a man raised from obscurity by individual kindness, and then, as narrow minds always incline, directed to exalt his own importance at the cost of minds far higher than his own genius, and less, infinitely less, tortuous in conduct.' II: 199-200.

When howling winds and louring skies,
The light *untimber'd* bark *surprize*,
  Near Orkney's boisterous seas;
The trembling crew *forget to swear*,
And bend their knees, unused to prayer,
  To ask a little ease.[119]

For ease the Turk ferocious, *prays*,
For ease the barbarous Russe, — for *ease*,
  Which P— could ne'er obtain,[120]

Which Bedford lack'd amidst his store,[121]
And liberal Clive with mines of ore,[122]
  Oft bade for — but in vain.[123]

For not the liveried troops that wait
Around the mansions of THE GREAT,
  Can keep, my friend! aloof
Fear; that attacks the mind by fits,
And Care, that like a raven *flits*.
  Around the lordly roof.[124]

---

[119] The surprize in which a light-timbered, or as *the Poet* has it a *light-untimbered* bark must be in when overtaken by a storm is most happily expressed. The sailors forgetting their oaths is a fine conception. In the concluding lines, the returning sounds of *seas, knees,* and *ease,* so near together, have a pretty effect upon the ear. [Beckford's note].

[120] Gifford's text reads P___k for Palk, that is, Sir Robert Palk (1717-1798), governor of Madras. By leaving off the 'k', Beckford allows the initial 'P' to stand for Pitt.

[121] Francis Russell, 5th Duke of Bedford (1765-1802), entered Parliament as a Whig and became a supporter of Charles James Fox (1749-1806) and a critic of Pitt. He protested against Pitt's suspension of the Habeas Corpus Act in 1794. Despite his great wealth, his initial forays in the House of Lords were marked by nervousness and an awareness of his own educational deficiencies, which he later overcame. He must have been aware of this reference to him since his personal copy of *Modern Novel Writing* has survived and is one of the four copies owned by Yale (Beckford 88).

[122] Robert Clive, 1st Baron Clive (1725-1774), as governor of Bengal 1755-1760 and 1767, he helped to establish British power in India. But, when he returned to England as a man of wealth, he was before long accused of corruption in office. His life thereafter became marked by persistent unease. He had to defend himself in Parliament and, though vindicated, he suffered from depression, poor health and an opium addiction, and ultimately committed suicide.

[123] The two last lines of the first stanza end with the words, *prayer* and *ease,* and the two first of the second stanza end with *prays* and *ease,* (or rather Hibernice *aise*) which is beautiful in the extreme. The idea of putting *ease* up to auction, and making Lord Clive an unsuccessful *bidder,* is certainly original—it is grand—it is sublime. [Beckford's note].

O well is he; to whom kind Heaven
A *decent competence* has given.
   Rich in the blessing sent;
He grasps not anxiously at more,
Dreads not to use his little store,
   And *fattens* on content.

N.B. A contented mind is a continual feast, and continual feasting makes a man fat.

O well is he! for *life is lost.*
Amidst a whirl of passions *tost;*
   Then why, *dear Jack*, should man
Magnanimous ephemera! *stretch*
His views beyond the narrow *reach.*
   Of his contracted span?[125]

Why should he from his country run,
In hopes beneath a foreign sun
   Serener hours to find?
Was never man in this *wild chace?*
Who changed his nature with his place,
   And left himself behind.[126]

---

[124] The *liveried troops* here mentioned, mean *livery servants*, and not *fencible regiments*,—THE GREAT, means all titled and rich men in general, which brings to our mind a couplet, written by a lady.

I have no desire to reflect on *the state.*
But little Lord Montford is one of THE GREAT.

The happy mode of expression—Can keep, my friend! aloof fear! is most charmingly melodious, and the representing the raven *flitting* about the lordly roof like a bat, is new, and beyond all praise. Surely Gray should have written,

Far far aloof the *bat* affrighted sails.

Such appropriation of *non appertaining* properties gives an exquisite beauty to poetry. [Beckford's note]. Lord Montford would be Thomas Bromley, 2nd Lord Montford of Horseheath (1732-1799). Gray's actual line from 'The Bard', I. iii, l. 37 was 'Far, far aloof the affrighted ravens sail.'

[125] The idea of the Magnanimous Ephemera stretching his *views* beyond the narrow reach of his *span*, is worthy of Homer. [Beckford's note].

[126] A chace to find serene hours, is very well hit off indeed, common sportsmen find their game first and chace it afterwards, but here the chace is to find—this is superior to any thing extant. [Beckford's note].

For winged with all the lightning's speed,
Care climbs the bark, Care *mounts the steed*,
    An inmate of the breast.[127]
Nor Barca's heat, nor Zembla's cold,[128]
Can drive from *that pernicious hold*,
    The too tenacious guest.

They, *whom no anxious thoughts annoy*,
Grateful the present hour enjoy,
    Nor seek the next to know:
To lighten ev'ry ill they strive.[129]
Nor, ere misfortune's *hand* arrive,
    Anticipate the *blow.*[130]

Something must ever be amiss,
Man has his joys; but *perfect bliss*
    Lives only in the *brain*;
We cannot all have all we want
And chance unask'd to THIS may grant,
    What THAT has begg'd in vain.

WOLF rush'd on death in manhood's *bloom*,[131]
PAULET crept slowly to the tomb;[132]
    Here BREATH, *there* FAME was given;[133]
And that wise power who weighs our lives
By *contras* and by *pers* contrives [134]
    To make the balance even.

---

[127] An inmate of the breast mounting a steed, is good. [Beckford's note].

[128] Barca is an ancient Greek colony; Nova Zembla island is located off the coast of northern Russia.

[129] i. e. Those who are not annoyed by any ills strive to lighten them. Good again! [Beckford's note].

[130] That a *blow* should necessarily follow the *arrival of a hand* few persons would anticipate.—A *word* and a *blow* we have heard of.—This passage therefore denotes genius. [Beckford's note].

[131] James Wolf (1727-1759), celebrated British general, who died leading the assault on Quebec city at the age of 32.

[132] Possibly Harry Powlett, 6th Duke of Bolton (1720-1794), a British admiral, who lived a much longer life and was not as highly regarded a military figure as Wolf.

To THEE she gave *two piercing eyes,*[135]
A body—just of Tydeus' size,[136]
   A judgment sound and clear,
A mind, with various science *fraught,*[137]
A liberal soul and threadbare *coat,*
   And forty pounds a year.

To ME, one eye, not over good,
Two sides, that to their cost have *stood,*[138]
   A ten years hectic cough.
Aches, stitches, all the numerous ills,[139]
That swell the dev'lish Doctor's bills,
   And sweep poor mortals off:

A coat more bare than thine, a soul
That spurns the croud's malign controul,
   A fix'd contempt of wrong;
Spirits *above* affliction's *pow'r,*
And still to charm the lonely hour,
   WITH NO INGLORIOUS SONG! [140]

---

[133] Breath here means length of days, which has the recommendation of novelty. *Fame* instead of *breath* is a grand conception. [Beckford's note].

[134] This is surely one of the finest lines in the English language.[Beckford's note].

[135] How prettily complementary to his friend! [Beckford's note].

[136] According to Greek legend, Tydeus was the son of Oneneus, king of Calydon. He took part in the Seven Against Thebes and, though small in stature, distinguished himself as a powerful warrior.

[137] *Fraught* and *coat* are allowable rhimes. [Beckford's note].

[138] *Stood,* here means *withstood*—for two sides standing a cough, might otherwise be deemed harsh. [Beckford's note].

[139] It has generally been supposed that *the medicines* taken swelled the devilish Doctor's bills, but it is here evident they are swelled by *diseases.*[Beckford's note].

[140] The author's description of himself elucidates his own character, in the happiest and most fortunate manner. Every body must surely respect and honor a man who gives it under his own hand, that his soul spurns the *malign controul* of the croud, that he has a fixed contempt for every thing wrong, that his chearfulness can subdue affliction, and that he can sing like a nightingale to charm the lonely hour. This it must be acknowledged is indeed a *glorious song*!!! [Beckford's note].

Mr. Gifford having finished the reading of this excellent production, received the congratulations of the company, with a modesty peculiar to himself. Their applauses were long and reiterated, which encouraged him to bring forth another performance, written as he said in his younger days, 'Upon the pleasures of malignity.' [141] But the attentive Arabella perceiving his drift, incontinently snuffed the candles, and the servant at the same moment informing them that supper was on the table, all parties were satisfied, and every body becoming jocose, the evening was concluded with the utmost festivity.

It happened that a mastiff dog which Arabella had brought up from a puppy, had gone mad the preceding day. She therefore was afraid to indulge any further speculations on Henry's fate for the present. After a long night passed in the utmost disquiet, she arose with the lark, and determined to set out on a pilgrimage of love to find the dear object of her affections, if he still existed an inhabitant of this globe. Dressing herself therefore in a green Joseph which had been made for her grandmother, and tying a little straw hat upon her head, she set off with a shepherd's crook in her hand, and her pockets full of turnips.

---

[141] A variant text of *Modern Novel Writing* has 'Upon a Cobler's lapstone' for this phrase. See the section on 'Textual Notes' for Beckford's additional emendations.

XVI

A Meeting of Ectasy

Henry Lambert had constantly pursued the grand object of his enquiries, and had never relinquished a moment the fond hope of being united to the lovely Arabella. Ardent in all extremes, he found the dear idea vivify his heart. Early in the morning he was leading his high scented hounds to cover, and when evening cast her faded gloom over the face of nature, his library was his unfailing resource, while his cultivated mind trod the various paths of science with indefatigable perseverance. How long he might have continued in this tranquil state, it would be difficult to ascertain, and how frequently his sighs arose in contemplation of his loss, it might be equally impolitic to describe. But the result was ever advantageous to his feelings, and his honour in every conflict remained not only unimpeached, but even more conspicuous than before.

Henry's maternal uncle who was very feeble and infirm, was also a Peer of the Realm, with the rank of an Earl; and should his Lordship die without issue, it was evident that an ancient barony would descend to him in right of his mother. This therefore cheered his drooping spirits, as he trusted the time might not be far distant, when he should be able to come forward with that rank and dignity, which would establish his former pretensions to the divine Arabella.

While Henry remained in this situation of suspence, he received intelligence of his mother's death, who departed this transitory life in the middle of a rubber of whist, with Lady Di Danvers, Lord Ginger, and Colonel Sash.

No sooner had he heard the fatal news, than he mounted his best hunter and rode forward to the cottage of Arabella, that he might discover how far his expectations were likely to be realized in the possession of that excellent young Lady.

In the mean time Arabella had got a violent swelled face, by sitting out all night to listen to the mournful song of the nightingale, whose gentle warblings were echoed from grove to grove, and sweetly floated on the balmy zephyr to sooth her ravished ear.

All was still as death, the watch dog was silent in the yard, and the owl was mute in the aged oak, when she suddenly started from the bank of violets, on which she was reposing, and exclaimed, 'O Heavens! was that a spirit passed me?' Henry now rushed forward, and seizing the enchanting Arabella by the hair, thus tenderly expressed himself; 'O matchless effervescence of human happiness, divine empress of my soul, I have languished for ages to behold thee, I have been burnt up and consumed by the unquenchable fire of exhaustless passion. Every moment that passed, seemed to me to have the duration of a century. The sports of the field were vain in thy absence. I seemed like a forsaken doe on the banks of the Tigris. The golden glory of the sun when darting his meridian splendor on the sycamore shade, had no solace for my distracted heart. In sleep, the dainty visions of thy loveliness, played on my secluded senses, and irritated my hopes to the madness of despair. There was no music in the murmuring of the silver rivulet that babbled through the flowery brake; the pale moon glared on me with the dimness of death. O Queen of all my wishes, O incomparable Arabella, O thou most beautiful of the human race, what will become of me, if your frowns should fall upon me! one kiss from thy sweet lips would raise me to a height of joy, that the proudest earthly potentate never yet experienced in his gilded palace, or his outrageous ministers in the wide plunderings of official power. Wilt thou be mine, wilt thou bless thy Henry by accepting his proffered hand? Wilt thou become myself, the chief portion of my being, the light of my eyes, the rapture of my soul? I will hug thee to my heart, 'till it burst with extasy, I will play with the tangles of thy hair till faintness overshadows me.' To this eloquent rhapsody, the mild and invincible Arabella prepared a suitable reply. She had nearly eat up all her turnips, and therefore looked at him with commanding sweetness, while she said, 'To be the object of the adoration of such a mind as thine is, my Henry, of itself sufficient to raise the most humble to the pinnacle of human greatness! The tone of thy melodious voice falls on my nerves, like the calm operation of opium on the wretch in pain. Sweet Henry, pretty youth, fine gentleman! I will, I will be thy wife, immediately—let no time intervene till we are ONE. I have waited a long while, and began almost to be out of patience—therefore let us lose no more time—had we been married on our first acquaintance, at this period we might have been the parents of two girls and a boy, I am sure we might—here is my hand, take it and welcome.' She then sang gaily,

> Away to the church, to the church lead away,
> And to morrow at furthest, be our wedding day.

The enraptured lovers now returned hand in hand to the elegant cottage of Arabella, where orders were immediately given to prepare every thing necessary for the happy nuptials. Margaret Grimes was ready to jump out of her skin for joy—the old dog looked piteously upon them, and the villagers met in the neighbourhood to talk the matter over, and to get drunk with decent delight in honour of their good patron's felicity. Doctor Dedrick procured a licence, and the clerk bought a new wig upon the occasion, while Sir Timothy Rattlesnake offered generously to give her away. This kind proposal was instantly acceded to, and the next morning was fixed for the celebration of the holy rites of Wedlock. Henry and Arabella passed the evening alone in mutual endearments—a roast fowl, eggs, and spinnage for supper, he drank three pints of port, to prove the fervency of his passion, and she toasted his health in liberal potations of gin and water. Two happier beings never lived upon earth—they danced, they sung, they romped, till midnight, when with engaging gravity they separated to go to bed, and to dream of the delights of the coming day. The only unfortunate event was that Henry had forgot his night-cap.

XVII

A Wedding

In the morning Arabella appeared more blooming than the vernal rose, when bathed in the glittering dew of May. She was dressed in a pale sea green spencer, elegantly trimmed with blue flowers and gold spangles, her petticoat was of lilac silk covered with a yellow gauze, that produced the most beautiful effect. Her lovely locks were bound with a fillet of scarlet sattin, mixed with straw and artificial nettles, and her enchanting arms, bare above the elbow, fascinated the eyes of every observer—her shoes were pink ornamented with white roses and silver spangles—she appeared a perfect divinity, her smiles, her dimples, her soft looks of pathetic languor, were very much applauded, as Henry led her to the altar. We have in a former part of this work described his person, we therefore shall only now say that he was fashionably attired in boots and leather breeches, and a rough great coat with nineteen capes. The clergyman went through the ceremony with great decency, though Arabella was so much agitated that she hardly knew how to keep her countenance. The clerk having a cousin in the pay office rather gave himself more airs than the circumstances could justify, but every body admired Arabella's unaffected attire and virgin modesty. Henry looked grave at times, and a silent tear stole down his cheek not entirely unobserved, for a farmer's man stept up to him with great caution, and in a whisper informed him, that he had found a hare sitting, this a good deal disconcerted the Doctor, who shook his wig with disdain, and eagerly enquired, if there was any extraordinary news from the Continent. They therefore hastily returned home when a sumptuous entertainment was prepared which all the Militia regiments were invited to partake of.

After dinner Arabella, at the earnest request of Captain Malmsbury, favoured the company with the following song, which penetrated the hearts of all the spectators.

> Ah well-a-day!
> It is not now the month of May,
> Yet let us all be gay,
> Ah well-a-day!

Yes, we will sing
The praise of every living thing,
And for each other we will bring
The flow'rs of spring.

Ah well-a-day!
I must not sport with virgin play,
I'm married as they say,
Ah well-a-day!

This charming song received the most animated applause from all the company, particularly from Serjeant Tomlinson, who declared he would rather be Henry than an Ensign. At eleven o'clock precisely, Arabella was led weeping to her chamber, and a quarter before twelve, Henry flew to her longing arms and found all his fondest expectations realized in the possession, of youth, beauty, innocence, and love. The remainder of the party kept it up till a late hour and then marched off at open files, singing in a grand chorus, 'Britons strike home.'

Nothing ever equalled the bliss of Henry and Arabella, they passed their time in the sweetest reciprocity of affection, till at the end of six months, his fair wife presented him with a lovely boy, that consolidated their affections, and gave new interest to their existence. The babe was constantly in the arms of Henry, who seemed to transfer a part of his adoration for Arabella to the dear little innocent, who early discovered symptoms of the most surprizing genius, and grew fatter and more thriving every day, notwithstanding that in one year it had the jaundice, the measles, the whooping-cough, the small pox, the chicken pox, the nervous fever, the rickets, the mumps, the pleurisy, the stone, the gout, the bilious cholic, the dropsy, and St. Anthony's fire.

XVIII

A Melancholy Incident

Henry had gone to London on particular business, and had not written to his dear Arabella, for more than three weeks, when one evening, full of the idea of her beloved husband, she wandered to an adjacent grove, and seating herself under a sweet-briar, on a bank of camomile, at the very entrance of an old hermitage, she thought she heard the distant trampling of horses' feet. She listened,—in an awful solitude, seemingly sacred to silence every sound excites attention; again she listened, and took off her gloves. The grove with which she was surrounded obstructed her view, but the horseman whoever he was, she was now convinced drew nearer.

'Could it be her Henry?' she softly exclaimed: 'O no! that is impossible, he cannot yet have even left London.'

But gentle reader! think of her astonishment when she saw not indeed her Henry, but Mr. Peter Perkins (for it was he) leap from his horse, and with a lover's speed, for he had descried her from the avenue, fly to the romantic little spot, on which she was seated! He fell at her knees;—she fainted in his arms.

'O my Arabella! 'tis thy Perkins, my angel look up. What has my rashness done?—I was to blame to take thy softness unprepared!'

She now began to revive, when withdrawing herself gently from his arms, she softly exclaimed, 'O Mr. Perkins how could you surprize me thus?'

A tender conversation now ensued, in which Mr. Peter Perkins said all that the most honourable passion could dictate (for he was ignorant of her marriage with Henry) or the most refined generosity could suggest; and Arabella, (who was above the little affectations of her sex) readily acknowledged that her esteem for him was permanent and sincere. Mr. Perkins staid two hours in this sweet retreat, and in all that time the circumstance of her being already married never once entered her head. So true it is, that *love* absorbs all other considerations. He informed *his* Arabella he was going to the house of a friend, only a few miles distant, and that he should, with her permission, visit her frequently.

The moon now beginning to rise in all the beauty of 'clouded majesty'[142] warned Mr. Peter Perkins to depart, which he immediately did; whilst the lovely Arabella slowly walked towards her cottage, and before she had readied it, the idea of her present situation intruded on her thoughts, and banished every pleasant reflection.

'Why,' said she, 'did I not think of this before? why did I indulge a softness that must be suppressed? Ah tyrant love! those who sincerely feel thy power too often sacrifice every other consideration to thy all-ruling sway.'

Arabella who, however, as to worldly prudence was in general a very discreet person, thought it proper to write a full account of this meeting, to her Henry, and at the same time to expedite a billet to Mr. Peter Perkins, telling him that as she was now married, she never could desire to see his face again.

It was now the anniversary of little Tommy's birth-day, the darling of Henry and Arabella. He had attained his fourth year, and was the delight of the whole village. The prattling innocence of that age of beautiful simplicity, renders a child inexpressibly engaging. This lovely boy was particularly so. His delighted mother had written to her beloved Henry to conjure him to return home on that day. 'My dear it is our Tommy's birth-day.'

Arabella dressed the sweet boy in a new little green vest,[143] she had made on purpose for this day. 'It is your birth-day, my lovely Tommy.' Having said this she kissed him, and sent him out to play on a small green plat before the door, and then began to busy herself in preparing dinner.

Tommy for once had transgressed his bounds, and with another little boy about his own age had run after a beautiful goldfinch, which flew directly to a rose-bush, that hung over a running brook at the bottom of the garden. The lovely boy now attempted to climb the small twigs of a willow tree, whose branches were united with those of the rose-bush; but Ah gentle reader! how shall I relate the miserable event? The branch of the tree, too feeble for his weight, gave way, and he fell at once into the brook, which was wide and rapid, and the poor babe was sunk in a moment! By the rapidity of the stream the body was carried down to a small bridge, a few yards distant from where the accident had happened. The particulars of this unhappy event were afterwards gathered from his little play-fellow afore-mentioned.

---

[142] Milton, *Paradise Lost*, Bk. IV, l. 607.

[143] The description of Henry and Arabella's 'sweet boy in a new little green vest,' appropriately named 'Tommy,' appears to be an allusion to Henry Fielding's account of the innocent Tom Jones as a child. The account of Tommy's effort to save a goldfinch that follows also alludes to Tom Jones' attempt to rescue Sophia's little bird, leading to the breaking of a tree branch under his weight and his collapse into the water. *Tom Jones*, ed. Sheridan Baker (New York: W. W. Norton, 1995), 29, 54, 104–5.

Here I must lay down my pen to give vent to the tears of sacred pity, which fill my eye, when I reflect on the piteous fate of this sweet innocent.

But alas! what language can I find to describe the following afflicting circumstance? the tender father was now returning home, with joyful haste to partake of the chearful repast which Arabella had promised to prepare for their darling Tommy's birth-day; when in passing over the bridge, which led to his garden, he espied floating on the brook, the garment, the little green *vest* of his dear child. Breathless with affright, he plunged into the stream, and drew the poor babe from the rushes and sedge: But ah! cruel, miserable event! he saw his lovely eyes were now closed in death! he saw he was deprived of life! a pallid hue had already taken possession of those coral lips! His cheeks which wore the bloom of the opening rose, were now changed to the livid tints of death! Where now were those sweet smiles, which never failed of conveying transport to the delighted parents? Alas! gone, gone, gone!

'Gracious Heaven!' said the distracted father, 'what do I see! My Tommy! Is it, can it be possible? Ah, yes! O ye Powers support me!' He clasped the breathless infant to his bosom in all the agonies of frenzy and despair.

O reader! I cannot proceed.—A few moments just to wipe away the gushing tear, and then I will go on.[144]

Mr. Lambert whose agonies for what his beloved wife would feel on this dreadful occasion, was distracted how he should break the fatal story to her; and what still made it the more dangerous, the doating mother of this sweet babe, was now very far advanced in a second pregnancy; every precaution was therefore necessary.

He wrapped the breathless little corpse under his coat, and with almost frantic steps, conveyed it by a private staircase up into a remote chamber, in the further part of the house. He laid him on the bed, and once more kissed his pallid lips. Then in an agony of despair, which no language can describe, with hasty steps, on hearing his beloved Arabella call him to dinner, he ran down stairs. His agonies were still increased, when he saw the chearful innocence, the sweet smiles of that lovely woman, who had learnt his arrival from Margaret Grimes who had seen him enter.

'My Henry (she said with the most lively joy, and with an angel's sweetness) welcome, thrice welcome home. But where is our dear boy, where is Tommy? He is playing I imagine, on the green plat before the house. Call him my love

---

[144] A parody of Fielding's editorial intrusion through direct speech to the reader in *Tom Jones*, as in the case of the earlier statement notifying the reader that he had to 'lay down my pen to give vent to the tears of sacred pity, which fill my eye.'

to dinner. See, I have spread the table with our small repast, see his new little knife you sent him from London. I have laid it ready for him.'

Poor Mr. Lambert suffered at this dreadful period the utmost agonies. How loth was the tender husband, the affectionate parent, to disclose the horrid tale! How unwilling to disturb the tranquillity of his beloved wife, which was founded on an ignorance of the dreadful event.

Arabella with her usual sweetness, grew still more importunate.

'Say, my love, where is my Tommy?—Why my Henry will you not fetch the little truant to his dinner?' Henry could not stand this: he flung himself into a chair with an air of frantic wildness, and now began to weep aloud.

But here I must close the melancholy, heartfelt description. It will easily be imagined, the fond mother's anxious enquiries soon made her acquainted with the shocking fact. For several hours she remained in a state of absolute distraction. Her neighbours testified their kind affection by watching and attending her with the utmost care. The violence of her fits at length brought on the pangs of childbirth, and she was delivered a little before the usual time of another boy, even more beautiful than her Tommy.

Fortunately in a few hours little Tommy began to breathe again, and on the following morning was as merry and playful as ever. Mrs. Lambert also speedily recovered and before the expiration of three days was as well as could be expected. So that the happiness of this fond couple was restored to them with the *additional joy* of having another son.

XIX

A Conversation

It is a just observation of an author who well knew the human heart, that there is in *perfect beauty*, an attractive charm which is irresistible. Old Mrs. Mandrake turned pale, and sickened at the sight of so much innocent sweetness, and for once in her life, the well-bred assurance of a fine Lady forsook her for a moment only. She was heard to exclaim softly—'O Heavens! what bloom! what features!—Two of the gentlemen by an involuntary impulse, rose from their seats, and with a kind of homage to so much beauty, were going to lead Arabella to a seat next the fire; but Mrs. Mandrake, who had by this time recovered again her former insolence, cried 'Sit still Gentlemen, I beseech you,' then in a kind of scornful half whisper, 'Poor thing, she was a reputed orphan, but she has thought proper to marry a Gentleman forsooth!'

Arabella just heard the last syllable, and blushed a deeper dye, which still added to her beauty, she had been in tears too, and the lustre of her piercing eye, had now yielded to the softest languor. Well says the Poet,

> When beauty sorrow's livery wears,
>   We fondly take the fair one's part;
> But when loves shafts are dipt in tears,
>   They pierce directly to the heart.[145]

'Sit down Madam!' said Mrs. Mandrake. Arabella modestly obeyed her, and seated herself at the bottom of the room, and after a short time finding her Henry did not appear, she quitted the company.

---

[145] This is an air from Georg Friedrich Händel's musical drama, *Hercules* (1745), II, ii. Words are by Thomas Broughton (1704-1774). The actual lines sung by Dejanira, the wife of Hercules, are:

> When beauty sorrow's livery wears,
> Our passions take the fair one's part.
> Love dips his arrows in her tears,
> And sends them pointed to the heart.

The Gentlemen Instantly exclaimed 'Good Heavens! what a charming woman!' 'Such eyes!' said another. 'What an enchanting form!' another. Not one but was in raptures.

'Why I cannot say,' said Mrs. Mandrake, affecting to yawn with indifference, 'I cannot say I am so violently charmed with her person. I grant she has bloom, but it is the red and white of a milk-maid. She is, I think rather a *gawky* figure. Her arms are too long, and her eyes are horrid; she is tall I allow, and the picture of health, but she wants fashion, she wants elegance.'

Arabella tripped up stairs like a young roe, and taking her children alternately in her arms, cried, 'O how much has a mother to answer, who vain and proud, is above performing the sweetest of all duties, the improvement of her children's minds!

> Delightful task—
> To teach the young idea how to shoot,
> To rear the tender thought,
> To pour the fresh instruction o'er the mind,
> To breathe th' enliv'ning spirit; to implant
> The generous purpose in the glowing breast![146]

The next morning as Arabella was reading Euclid to amuse her infant progeny, and eating at the same time a buttered crumpit, Miss Slipshod rushed into the nursery, 'O Mrs. Lambert, what a discovery!' 'For Heaven's sake my dear,' said Arabella, half fainting, 'what is the matter?' 'My lovely friend,' replied the other, 'what do you think? A Mr. Ireland has discovered a trunk full of original manuscripts of the immortal Shakespere himself; it is as true as any thing; and there are besides two tragedies all written in blank verse, with old fashioned spelling, with double dds and double ees—and then there are I don't know how many love-letters in Willie's own hand writing, and a deed of gift to the finder of all that was in the trunk.[147]

---

[146] James Thomson, *Spring*, ll. 1152-6.

[147] William Henry Ireland (1777-1835), forger of Shakespeare's manuscripts. In 1794-5, he forged deeds and signatures relating to Shakespeare, letters to Anne Hathaway, which included a lock of his hair, created a manuscript of *King Lear*, which he said was in the dramatist's handwriting and even fabricated two plays as by Shakespeare, *Vortigern and Rowena* and *Henry II*. He claimed he found the cache in a trunk owned by an ancestor who had bequeathed it to him. 'Shakespeare MSS', *Monthly Magazine, or British Register*, I (February, 1796): 42-3. While he deceived many experts, Edward Malone attacked the authenticity of the documents in *An Inquiry into the Authenticity of Certain Miscellaneous Papers and Legal Instruments* published on 31 March 1796. Ireland confessed to the fraud shortly thereafter. Samuel Ireland, William's father and an avid collector, published *Miscellaneous Papers and Legal Instruments under*

Is not he a lucky man?' 'I think he is indeed,' returned Arabella; 'but my amiable friend, you cannot conceive how you alarmed me, I had nearly fallen into a fit, for by the hasty manner in which you expressed yourself, I really supposed, my valuable husband had broke his collar bone.'

---

the Hand and Seal of William Shakespeare in January 1796, sparking a debate over the authenticity of the manuscripts in the public arena. A number of Beckford's friends and associates took sides publicly on this issue. Revd Samuel Henley, Benjamin West, and William Hamilton (the artist) doubted the authenticity of the Shakespearian discoveries. Sir Isaac Heard was a believer. The Gentleman's Magazine, LXVI (April, 1796): 267 and (Supplement, 1796): 1101.

XX

Fine Discrimination of Character

It is one of the easiest things in nature to begin a novel the author as you may say 'Has the world before him where to chuse' [148]—but as the work proceeds, then comes the difficulty—

> Aye, there's the rub
> Must give us pause.[149]

Characters grow out of characters, fresh persons must necessarily be brought forward to heighten the interest, and as it approaches towards a conclusion, the plague is how to get rid of the good folks with decency—Some must be *married*, some must be KILLED OFF, and all must be properly disposed of. Never did any human being wish to get to the end of a journey with more impatience, than I (*my* Lady Harriet Marlow) do to finish this elaborate performance—I 'have taken arms against a sea of troubles' [150] and hardly know how to fight the waves any longer, for as my *prime* boast is precision, and my *second* consistency, so the ignorant reader can have no idea of the painful predicament in which I stand. 'ALLONS DONC,' as they say in France, there is now no retreat to be made—I must fight it out to the last, and so I will.

I trust, however, the speculative reader will pardon this digression, for in good truth *my Ladyship* does hate digressing, as it is flying from the subject, and of no use whatever, but to lengthen out the performance, for why should any body digress, unless he finds it of the greatest utility? *Intellect* like *bread* is every day getting more and more scarce, therefore we should make all possible shifts not to destroy the stock in hand. But to proceed.

---

[148] Milton, *Paradise Lost*, Bk. 12, l. 646. As Adam and Eve leave the garden of Eden, Milton writes: 'The World was all before them, where to choose.'

[149] Shakespeare, *Hamlet*, III, i., ll. 65-8.

[150] *Ibid.*, III, i., l. 59.

Henry Lambert was a gentleman—that is, he had wit, manners, and money,—by the bye, he had a fine house and park with all dignified appurtenances in Gloucestershire—but he preferred to live in Arabella's cottage, because it was so snug, and because Arabella was particularly fond of honeysuckles. I mention this to justify the meanness of his mode of living, for had he chose an establishment equal to GEORGE ROSE'S he could have afforded it, but never having held any office under government, he did not think it decent.[151]

Mr. Mandrake was a worthy man, many years older than his wife, had the misfortune to have a hump-back, and was usually laid up half the year with the gout. Mrs. Mandrake had been a very celebrated beauty in her youthful days, and was even still what might be called a fine woman; but *one* of her characters was (for most people have *two*) that of being proud and imperious to the utmost degree, besides which she was inordinately fond of oysters. Her worthy husband who still doated on her, and who feared her frowns so much, that he could hardly call his soul his own, indulged her in every fashionable excess. I mean so far as was consistent with the character of a woman of honour; for Mrs. Mandrake was, with all her faults, a woman of unblemished reputation; but she was tyrannical, proud and capricious to the last degree; what she liked to-day, she disliked to-morrow:—in short, she was quite a fine lady. She aimed at being thought a *wit* as well as a beauty; for which purpose her house, which was one of the most elegant in London, was the resort only of such as were celebrated for that character; and she was equally fond of speeches made to her *person*, as to her *understanding*. She had two daughters, whom, though nearly of the age of Arabella, she still kept upon the footing of children, as the very idea of having a daughter attending her to public places, and rivalling her in beauty, made her sicken with the dreadful apprehension of approaching old age. That celebrated observation of Monsieur St. Evremond might justly be applied to her, that 'the sighs of a fine woman at the hour of her departure, are more for the loss of her beauty than the loss of her life.' [152]

It was a lucky circumstance for this unnatural mother (and too many there are in the great metropolis of the same cast) that her two poor daughters (who were

---

[151] A reference to Rose's country house and estate called Cuffnells, located in Hampshire, which he was able to buy due in part to his friendship with Pitt, who gave him a lucrative post in the Court of Exchequer in 1784. Redding wrote that it was Rose's 'assiduity in serving his patrons through thick and thin' that got him into 'parliament and place.' Redding, II, 322.

[152] 'Of the Complacency that Women take in their Beauty,' *The Works of Monsieur de* St. *Evremond*, trans. Mr. Des Maizeaux (London, 1728), I: 153. The actual lines are: '… and if her sickness goes as far as death, the last sigh that goes from her, is more for the loss of her Beauty, than that of her Life.'

extremely to be pitied) were remarkably small of their age: they had the appearance of girls about thirteen. Mrs. Mandrake taking the advantage of their size, used to call them at all times the *children*, and her *little ones*; so that a byestander would have imagined they had not reached even the above-mentioned age. They were closely confined to their nursery, in white frocks, and were never so much as permitted to sit with her, or dine at the same table; she would have fainted had girls of their age called her *mother*, before any of her fine gentleman visitants.

Poor Mr. Mandrake loved his daughters, but was absolutely afraid to shew his affection, and had long since lost his authority in the family. Mrs. Mandrake's invitation to Emily Smithson, and notice of poor Mr. Grogram, proceeded from no benevolent principle. That worthy man, who was himself all truth and sincerity, had not the least idea of the false politeness of a fashionable fine lady. When she invited Emily to come to her, she had no notion the old man, as she called Mr. Grogram, would part with her; therefore thought she ran no risque in asking her: besides the truth is, *pride* was at the bottom; as she, like many other fine ladies, took no small pleasure (though the mistaken would imagine it a *benevolent* principle) in having a poor dependent at her beck: to have one to *scold*, just when she pleased; and as a witty author remarks,

To keep a girl to fret upon.

Monsieur Rochefoucault's admirable maxim, that 'we do not always do charitable *actions*, from charitable *motives*'[153] was never more verified than in this instance of Mrs. Mandrake. She had no real design of advancing poor Mr. Grogram's fortune, and while that worthy but mistaken man, was rejoicing, that his dear niece was now on the road to London to a rich and benevolent friend, this strange woman would have sickened to death, if she had imagined that the little Welch girl, as she called her, was perhaps, that day, the most beautiful young woman in England, adorned with every virtue, and possessed of the choicest accomplishments. The friendship she had in former days professed for the amiable Mrs. Smithson had been long since obliterated; so much does the dissipation of this age of pleasures entirely eradicate from the heart every sentiment of honour and sincerity.

But it is now time to return to Henry Lambert, who having fully discussed the above-drawn characters, to Arabella—ordered his curricle, and arrived at the bull-baiting, without one single adventure, or 'hairbreadth scape'[154] on the road.

---

[153] François la Rochefoucauld, *Maxims* (1665), no. 409.

[154] Shakespeare, *Othello*, I, iii, l.136.

XXI

A Critical Moment

Farmer Green's cow had broke into Arabella's garden during the night, and had played the very devil—the pease were all trodden down, the onions rooted up, the spinnage annihilated, the turnips, carrots, and potatoes destroyed; in short, there was a 'careless desolation'[155] in every part. 'What must we do?' said Margaret Grimes, the big round tear trembling in her eye. 'I am sure,' replied Arabella with violent emotion, 'I know not how to act in this emergency; how unlucky, that such a *catastrophe* should have happened in my beloved Henry's absence. He is gone to the *bull baiting*, and the *cow* has *baited* us in revenge. I know but one measure to adopt and that is to bear the misfortune with becoming fortitude. Complaint is useless, we must therefore support what we cannot rectify.' To the truth of this observation Margaret Grimes assented, with engaging modesty, and the children were called own, to whom the whole affair was properly explained. Mr. Peter Perkins, who had never lost sight of his object, but whose love for Arabella encreased even to madness by the difficulties which had attended its progress, now approached the cottage of Arabella and sent a servant to offer any assistance in his power. A transient blush pervaded her cheek at this tender proof of his affection, but her duty to Henry triumphed over the tenderness of her heart, and she requested him to take some refreshment after his fatigue, making at the same time every proper acknowledgment for the intended favour.

Arabella now requested Margaret Grimes to examine minutely the depredations of the cow, and the good woman taking the hint, immediately retired.

No sooner did Mr. Perkins find himself alone with the dear idol of his soul, than he burst forth into a torrent of the most enthusiastic adoration. He kissed her hand with fervor, a thousand and a thousand times, which she endeavoured to withdraw in vain, he entreated her to promise him, that, in case any accident should happen to Henry, she would take him for her second

---

[155] Shakespeare, *As You Like It*, III, iii, l. 400.

husband. To this, his earnest request, she faintly replied, while her bright eyes were bathed in tears. 'O Mr. Perkins urge me no further, I scarce dare think upon the subject, but should the melancholy event you allude to ever take place, which may Heaven avert, I know not any person who possesses so large a portion of my esteem as Mr. Peter Perkins.' He now imprinted numberless kisses on her vermillion lips, and fondly entwining her arms round her lovely waist, called her his *future bride,* his good genius, his protecting angel. In short, he appeared half frantic with extacy of joy, when Henry's voice was heard in the hall, which in some degree moderated his transports, 'I wish,' said Mr. Lambert as he entered the room, 'that Farmer Green would take better care of his cow.' There was a comicality in the allusion that occasioned a general laugh, when Henry shaking Mr. Peter Perkins by the hand, said he was heartily glad to see him, and kindly asked him if there was any news? 'None in the world,' replied Mr. Peter Perkins with somewhat of an embarrassed air, 'None upon earth, none at all that I hear of, the papers are quite barren of late.—The cow I find has done a deal of mischief—Had you much sport at the bull baiting—Was parson Chesnut there—I meant to have been there myself, but was prevented going—but I fancy it grows late—I am after my time, I must be off, good day to you Mr. Lambert, good day to you Madam, I hope you will favour me with a visit the first opportunity—do—I shall take it kind, I shall indeed.' Having made his oration, he disappeared.

The fond and faithful Arabella now threw her snowy arms round Henry's neck, and welcomed him home with that winning tenderness which artifice can never feign. When dinner was over, and the children were brought in, Henry and Arabella gave way to those fine feelings which connubial tenderness alone can experience. At length Mrs. Lambert took her harp and gazing on her husband with fond delight in a most enchanting manner sung the following

Air

When you are absent all looks *drearly,*
    When you are absent I am sad,
Because I love my Henry dearly,
    When he is with me I am glad.

O then, unless you wish to grieve me,
    No more desert my circling arms;
It breaks my heart that you should leave me,
    The lord, the master of my charms.

Henry was so enraptured by this extemporary proof of Arabella's attachment and regard, that he jumped from his chair, played a thousand antics, rolled the children on the floor, drank a bottle of burgundy, and sung 'God save the king.' [156]

---

[156] The patriotic hymn that became the national anthem of the United Kingdom. It was first sung in 1745 in the Drury Lane Theatre but appeared in print in *Harmonia Anglicana* in 1702. Donald W. Krummel, 'God Save the King,' *The Musical Times* (March 1962), 159-60.

XXII

Conclusion

After several months passed in the retired pleasures of Arabella's cottage, Henry proposed going to London, that they night live in a style suitable to their fortune. Mrs. Lambert gave her consent, and in consequence his house in Grosvenor Square was ordered to be prepared for their reception. A service of plate was bought upon the occasion, a great number of servants were hired, and every thing was established on the most expensive footing. At half past eleven one Monday the Lambert family quitted their rural abode and proceeded in a coach and six to the metropolis, where they arrived in perfect health and safety on the Thursday following.

Their house soon became the resort of all the rich wits and fashionable company of high life. They gave dinners, suppers, balls, assemblies and concerts to the amusement, gratification, and edification of all their acquaintance; Henry and Arabella became amazingly fond of deep play, and being remarkably lucky, won immense sums of money which raised them very much in the good opinion of the great. The children were educated in the utmost refinement, and with the most salutary delicacy, and discovered uncommon penetration and acuteness in all their studies. Dr. Grampus, their tutor, pronounced them to be the two most astonishingly clever boys, he had ever met with, and as he made it a rule never to restrain them in any of their little desires, so he became a wonderful favourite with them both, as well as with Papa and Mamma.

Arabella whose exquisite beauty was the admiration of all the young men of rank acted on every occasion with such guarded circumspection, that though some envious ladies of her acquaintance thought, or pretended to think, that she was rather *too particular* with Lord Kissville, yet they could not throw the slightest imputation on her character.

Mr. Peter Perkins followed the enchanting Arabella to town, and for some time frequented her assemblies 'sighing like furnace' [157] but as he was little

---

[157] Shakespeare, *As You Like It*, II, vii, l. 148.

acquainted with the forms and appearances of high life, he soon became contemptible in her eyes, in a short time, therefore, she so completely cut him, that he quitted the pursuit in anguish and dismay, execrating in the bitterness of his heart, the follies and vices of Aristocracy.

Amongst the number of elegant acquaintance which Mrs. Lambert had formed, was Lady Maria Jones, who though more advanced in life, treated Arabella with the utmost intimacy. One day Lady Maria was particularly melancholy; the frequent sighs she heaved, and the tears which bedewed her languid cheeks, affected the tender sensibility of Arabella in the greatest degree. She wept from the 'mere virtue of compassion,'[158] and gently asked, 'I hope my dear Madam no fresh affliction is the cause of these precious tears?' 'No, my Arabella, none, I have long been inured to misery;—my sorrows cannot be relieved but by death alone.' 'Would not,' said the amiable Mrs. Lambert, 'a participation of your griefs tend to lessen their weight? For when the heart is absorbed in affliction, and has long been accustomed to devour in secret its own griefs, it seeks not for relief, but gains strength by feeding on its own melancholy.'

'Alas my sweet friend,' replied Lady Maria, 'my sorrows are of a nature never to be redressed. You know, I imagine that I am married, that I am a mother, (though my dear little angel my Dicky is taken from me) that my husband, the husband of my tender youth (for I was early married) is now wandering in a foreign land with an infamous courtezan. All this perhaps you have heard, but methinks I read in my Arabella's eyes a kind curiosity to be further informed; a tender concern for the particulars of my unhappy story. I will gratify your desire, my Arabella, I will relate them to you, in hopes the recital may prove a warning to you in future life.— To begin then,

'I was left at the age of nineteen with a large fortune, when I became acquainted with Mr. Jones. His fine figure enchanted my sight, whilst the excellent qualities (as I imagined) of his heart merited my utmost regard: in fine I loved him to distraction. His passion for *me* appeared no less. No objection could possibly be made to the alliance, as his family was respectable though mine was noble, and his character was then good. But alas! it soon appeared his sole motive for marriage was my fortune only. The first three months of our union were spent happily; at least we were surrounded with so much company, and so many new scenes of dissipation presented themselves, that I saw not, what very soon was *too visible*, that the most perfect indifference had

---

[158] Shakespeare, *Tempest*, I, ii, l. 27. Prospero speaks of the 'very virtue of compassion' in Miranda.

taken place where I had 'treasured up my soul.' [159] This first began to appear, by his affecting to treat my understanding with much contempt, because I was a *woman*. If I ever in company gave my opinion on any reigning topic of discourse, he would cut me short with 'Good Heaven, my dear! How should a *woman* know any thing of these matters?' He very early began to launch into many extravagancies, particularly that of keeping race-horses. This I was acquainted with one day by seeing a beautiful horse exercising before the windows. On my asking him the occasion, he with a careless yawn replied, 'he intended him to run for the King's plate at Newmarket: but why,' added he peevishly, 'do I tell a *woman* of this?'

'But I was particularly hurt by his cruel behaviour to my aunt, a most worthy old Lady, who had bred me up from my infancy. From a hundred repeated slights, he at length absolutely forbid her the house, telling her the society of old women was intolerable. Soon after this, my dear boy was born. I wept in secret, I prest my innocent babe to my unhappy bosom, and was indulging a fond mother's hopes, that this little pledge of affection might touch his heart, when alas! that heart (but this I then knew not) was mine no longer.

'I tenderly loved my husband, notwithstanding these proofs of his indifference. We had then an elegant villa at Richmond, where I had lately become acquainted with a most agreeable young lady, a widow. She had lodgings very near me, and her company was so peculiarly pleasing to me, that I in some measure forgot my griefs; nay I even fancied my husband still loved me in his heart. I was perfectly charmed with Mrs. Ormsby, and found her cheerful conversation a great relief to my spirits. She had now been at Richmond near a month; Mr. Jones had been in London all that time. On his accidentally once or twice seeing her with me, and my expressing how much I esteemed her, he said he wondered greatly at my taste, for that he never saw a more disagreeable woman in his life; adding, whenever she is with you, I beg to know it, for her company I abominate. That afternoon he went with me

---

[159] From Charlotte Smith's verse, 'Intended to Have Been Prefixed to the Novel of Emmeline, But Then Suppressed.' Smith's novel *Emmeline* was published in 1788; this verse was originally entitled 'To My Children.' It was printed as the last poem in the first volume of the two-volume edition of *Elegiac Sonnets* (1795; 1797). See *The Poems of Charlotte Smith*, ed. Stuart Curran (New York: Oxford University Press, 1993), 95. The relevant lines are as follows:

> —May you, dear objects of my anxious care,
> Escape the evils I was born to bear!
> Round *my* devoted head while tempests roll,
> Yet there, where I have treasured up my soul,
> May the soft rays of dawning hope impart
> Reviving patience to my fainting heart;—

to drink tea with a family in the neighbourhood. I was in uncommon good spirits, as I fancied my dear Mr. Jones looked on me with more kindness than usual. Alas! how are we deceived! Mistaken mortals! About six o'clock we sat down to whist, all but Mr. Jones, who complained of a violent head-ache, and of a sudden recollected he had two letters to write, which he must send he said by the post that very evening.—'But my dear Maria,' he added (O how delighted was I with the kind epithet!) 'you will stay I hope the evening, I will order the coach for you at eleven; as to myself, when I have finished my letters, I shall retire to bed, for I feel myself somewhat out of order.'

'After he was gone I was extremely uneasy; I fancied (such was my tenderness for him) that he was more ill than perhaps he confessed, and as soon as the rubber was over, I told the Lady where I was, my fears, and that I would then go home, which was only in the next street. It was then about eight o'clock, and the season of the year delightful for walking at that hour. Accordingly I left the company, and was tripping home with great haste, when as I passed by Mrs. Ormsby's lodgings, I recollected a few words I had to say to her on a particular affair. I ran up stairs with my usual freedom, and seeing nobody in her dining-room, I at once opened her bed-chamber door; when, gracious Heaven! what was my amazement! I was almost petrified with astonishment. The first object I saw was my husband in bed with Mrs. Ormsby. I screamed with terror, and saw enough to be convinced she must be the most abandoned of women. She instantly, as indeed they both did, jumped out of bed, and escaped into an adjoining closet. My cries brought up the maid who gave me water and drops; and from her I gathered (for now all secrecy was at an end) that Mr. Jones had privately kept this base woman above a twelve month in London; that he had taken this lodging for her at Richmond, and that she passed for the widow of a late officer in the navy.'

As this *prosing* Lady was proceeding with her long story, Henry Lambert rushed into the room in a delirium of joy—'O my Arabella, my angel, my life! what do you think has happened, the greatest good fortune has come to us, we shall no longer wither in plebeian vulgarity—no my dearest wife—we are now *noble*—my uncle the Earl of Frolicsfun is dead, he is upon my soul, and I inherit the ancient barony of the family—I am now, *my Lord*, you are, *your Ladyship*—we shall have a coronet on our coach, and we shall have precedence, O what a glorious advantage it is to be a Lord, to sit in the House of Peers in one's robes, and to make fine speeches, and to be called the *Nubble Lud*—I think I shall run mad with pleasure.'

Arabella smiled with ineffable sweetness, and turning to her dear female friend, said 'well Madam is not this good news?' to which the Lady answered by a low courtesy and by politely congratulating their *ships* on their newly acquired honors, after which she took her leave with the most high-bred ceremony.

For the next fortnight their house was full from morning till night of persons of distinction, who came to pay their compliments to Henry and Arabella—both he and she were allowed to be remarkably *affable*, at the same time, that they knew how to support their *dignity* with propriety.

It was now announced in all the public prints that the Right Hon. the Earl of FROLICSFUN having died without issue, the earldom was extinct, but that the ancient barony of LAUGHABLE had descended to HENRY LAMBERT, ESQ. in right of his mother.

When the due period of external mourning was at an end, Lord and Lady Laughable were presented to their Majesties at St. James's, and were most graciously received.

To conclude, Lord and Lady Laughable continued to live together many years, tasting even greater happiness in each other, from the contrast which they had formerly experienced, esteemed and beloved by all who knew them and dealing out blessings all around them; and when death at last called them to regions of eternal bliss, they left behind them in their children, faithful representatives of their virtue and felicity.

FINIS

AN
HUMBLE ADDRESS
TO THE DOERS OF THAT EXCELLENT AND
IMPARTIAL REVIEW,
CALLED
THE BRITISH CRITIC.[160]

Ladies and Gentlemen,

As I am well assured that your invaluable criticisms on the various literary productions of the present day, proceed from the joint labours of many ingenious men, and respectable old women, so I feel myself deeply interested in your decision on the merits of the foregoing work. It is therefore my most ardent wish to deprecate your vengeance, it is my most anxious hope to obtain your praise.

O do not break a fly upon a wheel![161]

But surely I shall not be deemed too vain, or unpardonably presumptuous, when I express a lively confidence in your approbation of this my first essay as a novelist—I am certain I have spared no pains in the composition, and I have carefully avoided all those allusions and remarks which might tend to produce an overflow of your bile, or excite your laudable indignation. As I well know your noble natures never can forgive those scandalous sentiments of obsolete liberty, which our ridiculous ancestors were so eager to disseminate,

---

[160] The conservative, high Tory monthly. It began publication in May 1793 under the editorship of Nares and Beloe as a voice that would compete against revolutionary views and liberal discourse. This review presents a sustained work of Beckford's ironic treatment of this periodical's political and literary bias.

[161] Alexander Pope, 'Epistle to Dr. Arbuthnot', l. 138: 'Who breaks a butterfly upon a wheel?'

but which all moderate, honorable, and enlightened persons now hold in just execration and contempt; so my principal care has been to keep clear of all such subjects, as could give the slightest umbrage to your ingenuous minds, and extensive understandings. You also may conclude, that as far as silence gives consent, I perfectly approve of the two restraining bills which have lately passed into laws,[162] that I am a decided enemy to all improvement in political science, and wish to hear in the course of the ensuing campaign, that the British grenadiers shall have marched triumphantly into Paris.

But to return to my novel, I will be bold to say, that there is great precision and a pure moral tendency throughout the whole, with so inviolate a consistency of character, that I think I may challenge a fair comparison with any of my most celebrated competitors in the same line. The story you will allow to be plain, simple, interesting, well connected, and full of pathos; and I doubt not but you will think it worthy of your generous protection; nay, I even trust, that the wisest and most patriotic associators of the immaculate Mr. Reeves,[163] will be inclined to applaud its loyalty, and promote its circulation. Besides, as I have had the honor to inform you that it is the offspring of a female pen, I can rely with perfect satisfaction on the acknowledged gallantry of your gentlemen, and the tender sympathy of your ladies—indeed the more so, as I have the good fortune to be personally known to several very valuable members of your illustrious body, from whom have already received many striking proofs of justice, liberality and good will towards me.

Being convinced that you possess the most exquisitely refined taste in poetry, I have been particularly attentive to this article, which I trust will be deemed of prime quality, calculated for general benefit and immediate use, such as will neither clog your stomachs, nor produce that nausea, to which you are subject, upon taking any quantity of pungent, strong or stimulative rhimes.

If it should appear that I have occasionally borrowed a sentence or a thought from some of our most admired modern writers, I trust you will graciously forgive so venial an offence, as I am ready to affirm that any passages I may thus have selected, and transplanted, which shew to disadvantage in their new situations,

---

[162] The Treasonable and Seditious Practices Act and the Seditious Assemblies Act passed on 18 December 1795.

[163] John Reeves (1752?-1829), a government propagandist and informer. In November 1792 he established a Society for Preserving Liberty and Property against Republicans and Levellers. One of their goals was to discourage and suppress seditious publications. Werkmeister, 134-7. Redding described Reeves as 'the over-officious tool of the court' who was 'continually overacting his part ... He first endeavoured to distinguish himself by calling meetings to put down what he called republican principles—in other words, those of Mr. Fox and his friends, and was tried for a libel owing to his over zeal. He declared openly, that if parliaments were destroyed, the king would remain, insinuating he was all-sufficient.' Redding, II, 322.

were not inserted with a design of depreciating their excellence, but merely to display that happy intricacy of style and sentiment, without which no novel can have a just claim to your notice and approbation. With all humility therefore I am free to assert, that some of those extracts which unfortunately in my little work may seem ludicrous and absurd, possess great beauty and propriety as connected with their original combinations. If you should suppose that I have wished to excite a laugh at the expence of their respective authors, your high mightinesses are mistaken, my sole intention having been, by a happy mixture of discordant parts, to produce a pleasing regularity, with a lively and captivating variety.

> Thus from dissentions concords rise,
> And beauties from deformities,
> And happiness from woe.[164]

I dare say your imperial majesties will pronounce this quotation to be inapplicable; but if you should, I can only say, that you do not comprehend me, and are not so clear-sighted as you ought to be, and as hitherto I have always been inclined to think you.

Do me the favor to erect your magnificent ears with attention while I recite to you a fable that shall fascinate you.

A screech Owl, an Ass, a Peacock, and a Boar, formed themselves into a, critical Junto to decide upon the harmony of the groves, and the modulations of the forest. The roaring of the Lion was voted *nem. con.* to be bombast, the neighing of the Horse vapid and jejune, the song of the Nightingale miserable affectation, and the notes of the Linnet, the Goldfinch, and the Lark, namby-pamby nonsense. In short, they unanimously agreed that, (not including themselves) no living creature possessed any genius, musical powers, or natural melody, but THE MULE; his voice and abilities, therefore, they candidly acknowledged to be capital. These four animals now endeavoured to convince all the beasts and birds that their decision was a just one, and that in consequence, the mule ought to be the hero of the day.

With your permission 'most potent, grave, and reverend Signors!'[165] I will defer the moral, and the application, to some more favorable opportunity.

But to lay aside all levity, it is impossible to deny that you waste your midnight oil, to save the present race from the horrors of licentiousness and the encroachments of philosophy, and when it is considered that

---

[164] William Whitehead (1715-1785), 'The Enthusiast An Ode' (1744), ll. 64-6.

[165] Shakespeare, *Othello*, I, iii, l. 76.

> The evil which men do, lives after them;
> The good oft lies interred with their bones[166]

your disinterestedness must be most striking, for posterity, perhaps, may not pay to the pious memories of you or your employers, those honors which you have so assiduously struggled to deserve. You will, however, during your lives, find sufficient consolation from the idea, that you have supported to the best of your abilities, the good cause of GENERAL RESTRAINT and that you have laboured in your vocation with unabated ardor. If indeed the reflections of the fallen Adam should occasionally cross your minds, who on contemplating the miseries he had prepared for his descendants exclaimed,

> Who of all ages to succeed, but feeling
> The evil on him brought by me, shall curse
> My head, ill fare our ancestor impure
> For this we may thank Adam.[167]

Yet a proper sense of the immediate good enjoyed, must stifle every sensation of remorse, while you rank in public opinion with the PITTS, the WINDHAMS, the DUNDASSES, the GRENVILLES, and the REEVESES of the day.

Go on then great and generous arbitrators of national taste! in your glorious and splendid career, direct the thunderbolts of your rage at the heads of those infamous and audacious libellers, who degrade literature by their free discussions, and philosophical remonstrances; and who even insult religion by their pernicious doctrines of toleration. Be it yours 'to stand in the gap' between error and truth, between vice and virtue, be it yours to shake a flaming scourge, and to chastize those literary monsters who dare to push their researches beyond the sacred line of demarcation you have drawn.

To your virtues, liberality, and candour, the whole nation can bear testimony, for I defy the most impudent of your detractors to shew a single instance amongst all your writings, where you have spoken favorably of any work that was base enough to vindicate the hoggish herd of the people,[168] that was mean enough to object to any measures of the present wise and incorruptible administration,

---

[166] Shakespeare, *Julius Cæsar*, III, ii, ll. 80-1.

[167] Milton, *Paradise Lost*, Bk. 10, ll. 733-6.

[168] An allusion to Edmund Burke's famous description of the restless masses in England and France as the 'swinish multitude' in *Reflections on the Revolution in France* (1790).

or that was cowardly enough to censure the just and necessary war in which the nation is now so fortunately engaged. No, ye worthy magistrates of the mind! you have exerted your civil jurisdiction with meritorious perseverance, and if at any time you have stepped forth as warriors to defend the exclusive privileges of the FEW, against the vulgar attacks of the MANY, your demeanour has been truly gallant, you have thrown your lances with a grace, becoming the most renowned knights of chivalry, and have hurled your anathemas at the murmuring multitude with a dignified fury that would have done honour to Peter the Hermit,[169] or to the chief of the Holy Inquisition.[170]

Owing to your animated exertions, and the vigorous measures of your *patrons*,[171] you may soon hope to see the happy inhabitants of this prosperous island express but one opinion, and act with one accord, the rich and the powerful shall be tranquilly triumphant, the low and the wretched patiently submissive, great men shall eat white bread in peace, and the poor feed on barley cakes in silence. Every person in the kingdom shall acknowledge the blessings of a strong regular government; while the absurd doctrine of the Rights of Man,[172] shall be no more thought of, or respected, than the rights of horses, asses, dogs, and dromedaries.

That your enemies may speedily be cast into dungeons, or sent to Botany Bay,[173] and that yourselves may become placemen, pensioners, peeresses, loan-mongers, bishops and contractors, is the constant wish and earnest prayer of,

Ladies and Gentlemen,
Your devoted humble servant,
HARRIET MARLOW.

THE END

---

[169] Peter the Hermit (d. 1115), revivalist preacher and leader of the People's Crusade that was marked by disorder, violence and the loss of numerous lives.

[170] Known as the ecclesiastical tribunal for the suppression of heresy and punishment of heretics, organized in the 13th century under Innocent III, under a central governing body at Rome called the Congregation of the Holy Office. *O.E.D.*

[171] i.e. William Pitt and other conservative supporters. It was believed that the *British Critic* was able to be launched initially because of backing from Pitt's secret service money and from Tory churchmen subscriptions . Derek Roper, *Reviewing before the Edinburgh 1788-1802* (London: Methuen & Co., 1978), 23.

[172] The revolutionary doctrines of Thomas Paine's *The Rights of Man* (1791).

[173] A penal colony in New South Wales, Australia that was to be established in 1788 by the British but, upon finding it to be uninhabitable, it was moved to Port Jackson, the site of Sidney today.

Textual Notes

George Robinson (1737-1801), in partnership with his son George Jr. (d. 1811) and his brother John (1753-1813), published *Modern Novel Writing, or the Elegant Enthusiast; and Interesting Emotions of Arabella Bloomville. A Rhapsodical Romance; Interspersed with Poetry* on 14 June 1796 in London. It went through one edition but was translated into German for publication in Weissenfels in 1798, under the title *Miss Arabella Bloomville. Ein Rhapsodisticher Roman von Lady Harriet Marlow.*

There is no record of how many copies Robinson printed, but only twelve copies of the English edition have been located so far. They are identified as follows: 1-4. Beinecke Library, Yale University, Im B388.796, copy1; Im B388.796, copy 2 (Michael Sadlier copy); Im B388.796, copy 3 (Beckford's personal copy); Beckford 88 (Francis Russell, Duke of Bedford copy); 5-6. British Library 12614. bb.15; G. 17958, copy 2 (Grenville copy); 7. Bodleian Library, Oxford University, Bodley 12 Θ 1164-1165 (Hodgkin copy); 8. Houghton Library, Harvard University, Ec8 B3884 796m; 9. UCLA, PR 4091. m72 (Samuel Rogers's copy); 10. Princeton University Library, 18th-31 (Robert H. Taylor's copy); 11. copy sold at H. Bradley Martin's Library sale, Sotheby's New York, April 1990, lot 2604; 12. Bernard Quaritch copy listed in catalogue 1132, October 1990, item 7.

Modern Novel Writing has been available in two facsimile reprint editions. The first of these, utilizing the Harvard copy, appeared in 1970 with a short introduction by Herman Mittle Levy, Jr. (Gainsville: Scholars' Facsimiles and Reprints); the second facsimile edition, reproducing Yale Im B388.796 (copy 1) came out in 1974 with a brief introduction by Gina Luria (New York and London: Garland). Neither of these publications provided any textual notes or scholarly apparatus. The most comprehensive critical and bibliographical work on this novel has been conducted by Deborah Griebel in her Ph.D. dissertation, 'A Critical Edition of William Beckford's *Modern Novel Writing* and *Azemia*' (University of Toronto, 1984). As part of her study, she collated nine copies of *Modern Novel Writing* and found a set of four 'fully corrected' copies (UCLA, British Library 12618.bb.15, Bodleian Library, Yale Im B388 796 copy 3). These changes involved cancelled and replacement leaves in the second volume, namely E6, 7, 8, 9, 11, 12 and G4, 5, 6 and 10, in order to include the pseudonyms Sam Slybore, Squares and Bilbo for Hoppner, Nares and Beloe along with appropriate variant changes to accommodate these alterations. (Griebel, xxxv-vi). She used the Hodgkin copy at the Bodleian Library for her edition.

For this edition, I have used Beckford's personal copy at Yale as the copy-text since this copy is one of the fully corrected examples of *Modern Novel Writing*, containing changes that Beckford himself must have approved. Following my own review of the text, I have made some changes that are listed below. It should be noted that my emendations are restricted to obvious errors in printing, punctuation and spelling. After examining all four texts at Yale and the Harvard copy, I also supply a list of forty-seven corrections Beckford made or approved as reflected in his personal copy of the novel. In the case of these emendations, I have included the page numbers of the original text where the changes were made on the right side. The page and line numbers for this edition appear on the left.

Editor's Emendations

Volume I:

Page	line	Editor's version	Beckford's version
36	17	in fine	infine
40	14	Colonel	colonel
41	7	too	two
42	4	changed, and	changed. and
45	34	present	pesent
48	14	through	throught
48	22	mistletoe	misletoe
52	17	Aspen	Aspin
55	40	paused —	paused ---
57	20	hypocritical	hyprocritical
59	16	fickleness	fickleness
65	11	at hand.	at had.
67	32	Peggy.'	Peggy.
69	23	time,	time;
69	27	roof	root
74	31	don't	do'nt
77	4	lichens	lickens
80	18	Barton —	Barton- -
89	24	convince	convince,
97	27	biting	biteing
99	24	it.'	it.
102	1	masquerade.	masquerade,
108	14	weeds,	weeds;

Volume II:

Page	line	Editor's version	Beckford's version
127	18	ma'am	ma'em
127	21	Haven't	Have n't
132	16	stifled	stiffled
133	6	having gagged her,	gagged her, having
134	1	Amelia	Arabella
134	24	Amelia	Arabella
141	35	breathe	breath
144	6	ignominy	ignomity
145	15	enchanting!'	enchanting!
146	5	tete-a-tete,	tete-a-tete.
147	12	cooked,	cooked;
147	14	hours:	hours;
148	6	herself in a blue	herself a blue
149	12	containing	con- containing
155	7	fat.	fat..
158	17	set	sat
159	17	pretensions	pretentions
160	38	immediately	im-diately
162	18-19	with great	withgreat
164	24	'who	who
168	2	irresistible	irrisistible
169	2	Not	not
169	12	minds!	mind!
169	20	crumpit,	crumpit.
170	1	'but	but
177	1	cottage,	cottage.
179	11	'But	But
179	18	'I	I
180	4	head-ache	head-ach
182	5	decision	dicision
185	2	bones	bones.
185	3	your	Your
185	15	stifle	stiffle

Beckford's Emendations

Volume II

Page	line	Beckford's changes	alternate version	page number of the original text
135	17	Squares	Nares	[II: 83]
136	4	Bilbo	Beloe	[II: 84]
136	12	Sam Slybore	my Hopner	[II: 84]
136	13	Sam Slybore	my Hopner	[II: 85]
136	14	twenty-four	twenty four	[II: 85]
137	3	Squares	Nares	[II: 85]
137	8	Squares	Nares	[II: 86]
137	8	love	love,	[II: 86]
137	10	Squares	Nares	[II: 86]
137	11	divine	Divine	[II: 86]
137	13	drooping	droping	[II: 86]
137	15	Review	British Critic	[II: 87]
137	6	Sam Slybore	my Hopner	[II: 87]
137	19	Bilbo	Beloe	[II: 87]
137	21	Squares	Nares	[II: 87]

Page	line	Beckford's changes	alternate version	page number of the original text
137	21	Sam Slybore	*my* Hopner	[II: 87]
137	23	Squares	Nares	[II: 88]
137	25	Squares	Nares	[II: 88]
137	27	the Painter	*his* Hopner	[II: 88]
138	1	**Ode to my Dear Square**s	**Ode to my Nostrils***	[II: 88]

Removed footnote *Lucinda, to avoid the imputation of pedantry, adopted the English word
Nostrils instead of the Latin *Nares*, and it certainly has a more poetical effect.[II: 88]

138	2	Squares! best formed	Nostrils! formed	[II: 88]
138	11	Sam Slybore's	*my* Hopner's	[II: 89]
139	7	Squares so	Nostrils dear	[II: 89]
139	19	Gifford,	Gifford	[II: 90]
139	21	Bilbo	Beloe	[II: 90]
139	22	Sam Slybore	*My* Hopner	[II: 90]
140	19	Squares	Nares	[II: 93]
140	20	correspond	corresponded	[II: 93]
141	14	Woodland	woodland	[II: 95]
141	35	breath	breathe	[II: 96]
142	2	winning smiles,	spectacles,	[II: 96]
142	2	whose voice	whose grin	
142	4	Squares	Nares	[II: 96]
152	15	tall, very short	fat, very thin	[II: 127]
152	17	yet	and	[II: 127]
152	17	round;	round,	[II: 127]
152	18	fly;	fly,	[II: 127]
152	20	fish;	fish,	[II: 127]
152	22	crow;	crow,	[II: 128]
153	8	Bilbo	Beloe	[II: 130] Harvard copy
153	9	Bradwell	Hook	[II: 130] Harvard copy
153	11	author	Author	[II: 130] Harvard copy
153	17	Square's	Nares's	[II: 130] Harvard copy
153	17	Sam Slybore	*my* Hopner	[II: 131] Harvard copy
157	4	fraught*,	fraught*	[II: 137]
158	4	days,	days.	[II: 139]
158	5	the pleasures of malignity	a Cobler's lapstone	[II: 139]

Selected Bibliography

I. Editions of *Modern Novel Writing*:

Modern Novel Writing, or the Elegant Enthusiast; and Interesting Emotions of Arabella Bloomville. A Rhapsodical Romance; Interspersed with Poetry. In Two Volumes. By the Right Hon. Lady Harriet Marlow. London: Printed for G. G. and J. Robinson. MDCCXCVI.

Miss Arabella Bloomville. Ein Rhapsodisticher Roman von Lady Harriet Marlow. Weissenfels: Severin, 1798.

Modern Novel Writing (1796) and *Azemia* (1797) By William Beckford Facsimile Reproductions with an Introduction by Herman Mittle Levy, Jr. Four Volumes in One Gainsville, Florida Scholars' Facsimiles & Reprints 1970.

Modern Novel Writing Or the Elegant Enthusiast William Beckford In Two Volumes with an Introduction for the Garland edition by Gina Luria Garland Publishing, Inc., New York & London 1974. Reprint edition.

'A Critical Edition of William Beckford's *Modern Novel Writing* and *Azemia*,' Ph.D. dissertation by Deborah Griebel, University of Toronto, 1984.

II. Works Relating to *Modern Novel Writing*:

A. Bibliography:

Chapman, Guy and John Hodgkin. *A Bibliography of William Beckford of Fonthill.* London: Constable and Co., 1930.

Gemmett, Robert J. 'An Annotated Checklist of the Works of William Beckford,' *Papers of the Bibliographical Society of America*, 61 (Third Quarter, 1967): 243-58.

Gotlieb, Howard. *William Beckford of Fonthill.* New Haven: Yale University Library, 1960.

B. Contemporary Reviews:

The British Critic, 9 (January 1797): 75-6.

Critical Review, 18 (December, 1796): 472-4.

English Magazine, 2 (1797): 134.

The Monthly Magazine and British Register, 3 (January, 1797): 47.

The Monthly Mirror, 2 (September, 1796): 286.

The Monthly Review, 20 (August, 1796): 477.

C. Other:

Alexander, Boyd. *England's Wealthiest Son A Study of William Beckford.* London: Centaur Press, 1962.

Bernard Quaritch Catalogue 1132, *English Books & Manuscripts.* London, 1990, 5-7.

'Biography of Eccentric Characters. William Beckford, Esq.,' *The Ladies' Monthly Museum*,' 19 (February, 1824): 67-71.

Black, Frank Gees. 'Burlesques of Epistolary Fiction,' in *The Epistolary Novel in the Late Eighteenth Century* (Eugene: University of Oregon, 1940), 97-100.

Chapman, Guy. *Beckford.* 2nd ed. London: Rupert Hart-Davis, 1952.

Darton, Eric. 'The Satirical Novels of William Beckford: 1. *Modern Novel Writing* (1796),' *Beckford Tower Trust* (Spring, 1990), 5-7.

Fielding, Henry. *The History of Tom Jones, A Foundling.* 4 vols. London, 1749.

Fothergill, Brian. *Beckford of Fonthill.* London: Faber and Faber, 1979.

Freeman, Arthur. 'William Beckford's *Modern Novel Writing*, 1795-6: Two issues, "Three States,"' *Book Collector*, 41 (Spring, 1992): 69-73.

Gemmett, Robert J. 'Excursions into Satire: *Modern Novel Writing* and *Azemia*,' in *William Beckford*. Boston: Twayne Publishers, 1977, 122-26.

_____. *The Consummate Collector William Beckford's Letters to His Bookseller*. Norwich: Michael Russell, Ltd., 2000.

_____. 'William Beckford's Authorship of *Modern Novel Writing* and *Azemia*,' *Papers of the Bibliographical Society of America*, 98 (September, 2004): 313-25.

Grimsditch, Herbert B. 'William Beckford's Minor Works,' *London Mercury*, 14 (1926): 599-605.

Hawke, Baroness Cassandra. *Julia de Gramont*. 2 vols. London, 1788.

Hervey, Elizabeth. *Melissa and Marcia; or the Sisters: A Novel*. 2 vols. London, 1788.

Keymer, Thomas and Peter Sabor. *Pamela in the Marketplace Literary Controversy and Print Culture in Eighteenth-Century England and Ireland*. Cambridge: Cambridge University Press, 2005.

Melville, Lewis. *The Life and Letters of William Beckford of Fonthill*. London: William Heinemann, 1910.

Moore, Thomas. *The Journal of Thomas Moore*. ed. Wilfred S. Dowden, vol. 1. Newark: University of Delaware Press, 1983.

Nolan, Jerry. 'Introduction,' *Edward and Ellen by William Beckford. Short Story as Prologue to Azemia in 1798*. London, 2007, 1-4.

_____. 'William, Elizabeth & William or Female Impersonation and Radical Satire,' *The Beckford Journal*, 6 (Spring, 2000): 35-45.

Oliver, J. W. *The Life of William Beckford*. London: Oxford University Press, 1937.

Parreaux, André. 'The Caliph and the Swinish Multitude,' in *William Beckford of Fonthill, Bicentenary Essays*. ed. Fatma Mahmoud. Cairo, 1960, 1-15.

Radcliffe, Ann. *The Castles of Athlin and Dunbayne. A Highland Story*. London, 1789.

Redding, Cyrus. *Memoirs of William Beckford of Fonthill*. 2 vols. London: Charles Skeet, 1859.

Richardson, Samuel. *Pamela or Virtue Rewarded* 2 vols. London, 1740.

Robinson, Mary. *Vancenza; or, The Dangers of Credulity*. 2 vols. (London, 1792)

Rogers, Samuel. *Recollections of the Table-Talk of Samuel Rogers*. New York: Appleton, 1856.

Rogers, Winfield H. 'The Reaction Against Melodramatic Sentimentality in the English Novel, 1796-1830,' *PMLA*, 44 (March, 1934): 98-122.

Shepperson, Archibald B. *The Novel in Motley A History of the Burlesque Novel in English*. New York: Octagon Books, Inc., 1967.

Smith, Charlotte. *Celestina*. 4 vols. London, 1791.

III. Secondary Sources:

Adams, M. Ray. 'Robert Merry, Political Romanticist,' *Studies in Romanticism*, 2 (Autumn, 1962): 23-37.

Blakey, Dorothy. *The Minerva Press 1790-1820*. London: Oxford University Press, 1939.

Clark, Roy Benjamin. *William Gifford Tory Satirist, Critic, and Editor*. New York: Columbia University Press, 1930.

Gifford, William. *The Baviad and Mæviad*. London, 1797.

Hargreaves-Mawdsley, W. N. *The English Della Cruscans and their Time, 1783-1828*. The Hague: Martinus Nijhoff, 1967.

Havens, Raymond B. *The Influence of Milton on English Poetry*. New York: Russell & Russell, 1961.

[Lettice, John]. 'William Beckford, Esq. of Fonthill,' *The European Magazine and London Review*, 32 (September, 1797): 147-50.

Mckay, William and W. Roberts. *John Hoppner, R. A.* London, 1914.

Piozzi, Hester Lynch. *British Synonymy; or An Attempt at Regulating the Choice of Words in Familiar Conversation*. 2 vols. London, 1794.

_____. *Thraliana: The Diary of Mrs. Hester Lynch Thrale (Later Mrs. Piozzi) 1776-1809*. 2 vols. ed. Katharine C. Balderston. Oxford: Clarendon Press, 1951.

Roper, Derek. *Reviewing Before the Edinburgh 1788-1802*. London: Methuen, 1978.

Rose, J. Holland. *A Short Life of William Pitt*. London: G. Bell, 1925.

Werkmeister, Lucyle. *A Newspaper History of England 1792-1793*. Lincoln: University of Nebraska Press, 1967.